THE ILLUSTRATED BOOK OF
Trees

THE ILLUSTRATED BOOK OF
Trees

A visual guide to more than 250 species

CONSULTANT EDITOR: **Dr. Eric A. Bourdo Jr.**

SALAMANDER

The Illustrated Book of Trees

Published by Salamander Books Ltd.
The Chrysalis Building
Bramley Road
London W10 6SP

© Salamander Books Ltd. 1999, 2003

An imprint of **Chrysalis** Books Group plc

2 3 4 5 6 7 8 9 10

Editor Polly Boyd
Design and layout Mick Hodson Associates
Filmset SX Composing, England
Colour separation P & W Singapore
Printed in China

CONTENTS

INTRODUCTION

WHAT IS A TREE? Although the concept of a tree is a familiar one, its exact definition is elusive. While it is possible to divide the Plant Kingdom into various groups by morphological characteristics, trees do not form one of these groups, but span many of them. Thus we cannot define a tree in the same way as we define, for example, a conifer, an oak or a beech. One convenient definition is to say that a tree is a woody plant growing on a single stem to at least six metres tall. We must consider, however, what we would call a tree of only five or even three metres tall, or one with two or even three main stems. As height decreases and the number of stems increases the plant becomes more like a shrub, defined as a woody plant with numerous stems arising from the base. But then what of a shrub with only two or even a single stem?

The fact that there is no clear definition between a tree and a shrub can be seen by looking at the way plants are grouped and named. Within a single genus the distribution of trees and shrubs varies. Many genera, such as Abies and Fagus, contain only trees, while others consist of a mixture of trees and shrubs. Oaks (Quercus) are best known as magnificent trees, but there are in fact many shrubby species, particularly in warm, dry areas such as California, and while most pines are large trees, several mountain species grow naturally as low shrubs. Conversely, some genera we know best as shrubs have less familiar tree members, for example Buddlejas making 10 m tall trees are found in Mexico and Central America.

At the species level, we may think we are safe in defining a tree. This, however, is not always the case. Many species that grow over a wide altitude range may form large trees low down but only low shrubs at high altitudes. In addition, some species which are normally trees can give rise to shrubby forms as shown by the numerous dwarf conifers cultivated in gardens, often the progeny of enormous forest trees.

THE WORLD'S FORESTS

It has been estimated that without man's influence, some 40 per cent of the land surface of the earth would be covered by forests, the only areas not dominated by trees being grasslands, tundra, the tops of high mountains and deserts. Forest types are extremely diverse depending on climate, but generally an increase in temperature and available moisture leads to an increased number of species. In the most northerly regions, where ground water is frozen for much of the year, trees need to be able to survive not only in conditions of drought as severe as in the desert, but also in extremely low temperatures. The evergreen, needle-like leaves of conifers, which lose little moisture, adapt them extremely well for this harsh environment and thus the most northerly forests consist of conifers such as Abies, Picea and Pinus. The same features also enable conifers to form forest further south, for example in high mountains and hot, dry regions where few other trees will survive.

Temperate forests contain a much greater diversity of species than do the northern coniferous forests. Here, with less harsh conditions to endure, trees can show a greater range of adaptations for competing with other plants for available light, essential for growth. Therefore broad, spreading trees abound here, densely covered with broad leaves. Typical trees of temperate forests include Carpinus, Fagus, Fraxinus, Tilia and deciduous Quercus. In temperate forests, flowering and fruiting is dictated by the seasons, so most trees flower in spring and fruit in autumn.

In warm temperate regions, such as the SE United States, more evergreen species such as evergreen Quercus and Pinus are found, while high rainfall gives rise to temperate rainforest as in Chile, with many Nothofagus, and in NW North America, where conifers such as Tsuga dominate. In warm dry regions with wet winters and dry summers, such as southern California and the Mediterranean, trees such as pines and evergreen oaks are adapted to growing in spring and surviving summer droughts.

Wet tropical forests occur around the equator in South and Central America, Central Africa, southern and southeast Asia and northern Australia. It is in these forests that the range of trees found is the most diverse, often with hundreds of different species in each square kilometre. Here, where water, heat and light are available throughout the year, and as there is no reason to shed leaves, except dead ones, trees are evergreen. They do not need to wait until winter has passed to flower, so flowering, and therefore fruiting as well, occurs throughout the year. The forests consist mainly of trees of different height. Some, known as emergents, tower above the rest, reaching heights of 50 metres or more. As little light reaches the forest floor, there is little ground flora, but epiphytes, such as Bromeliads, which grow on the branches of trees where they can reach the light, are common.

THE LIVING TREE

A carpet of acorns or beech nuts beneath a tree, or white fluffy poplar seed blowing in the wind, are both indications of a successful seed crop. A mature tree is capable of producing thousands of seeds, but not all of these will germinate, and not all of those that germinate will grow into mature trees. Like other plants, trees produce a large amount of seed to ensure that at least some of it is successful. For a seed to flourish it needs to be carried away from its 'parent' tree, as there is little point in trying to grow in dense shade, and to fall in a place where conditions are suitable for germination. So light seeds, such as those of maples, birches and poplars, are designed, by bearing hairs or wings, to be carried on the wind. Heavier seeds are attractive to feeding animals, which will carry them away, whether they are rowan berries eaten by birds or acorns gathered by squirrels.

Not all seeds blown in the wind will find a suitable place to grow. Only a small proportion are likely to find the perfect position. Those that are attractive to animals perhaps have an even less likely chance of success. Most will be eaten, some will be stored for later use and may or may not be found again, while others will be dropped accidentally while they are being carried away. Surprisingly, seed eaten by birds is often likely to germinate. The seed is usually resistant to the bird's digestive system, which in fact breaks down barriers on the seed designed to prevent germination.

Most seeds of temperate trees germinate in spring, when conditions are suitable. Even if dispersal and germination have been successful, a seedling will soon have to compete with others for the light and nutrients it needs. Where numerous seedlings are germinating together only the strongest will survive. They soon overshadow the others, taking all the available light, while the weaker seedlings remain stunted and eventually die.

Without an open space in the canopy, even the strongest seedling can remain stunted, or at best be tall and spindly. In a natural forest, however, where trees are all of different ages, there are always some near the end of their life. As a result of the deterioration of these older trees, more light will penetrate their thinning foliage, thus allowing young saplings to grow. When the old trees eventually fall, younger ones will be ready to take their place. Given ample light the young tree can now grow strongly to reach the canopy and spread its head to fill the space left by the recently fallen tree.

As a tree grows it starts to lay down wood internally. Wood is necessary for two reasons. Firstly to support the enormous weight of a mature tree, and secondly to conduct sap from the roots to the young growing tissues. The light springwood, formed early in the year contrasts with the darker summerwood, formed late in the growing season. This creates the annual growth rings enabling a cut trunk to be dated according to the number of rings it bears. Externally a layer of bark is produced, which can be so characteristic for each tree that it aids identification. Bark serves to protect the delicate tissues just beneath from damage by animals, fungi, desiccation, frost and even forest fires.

Young trees will often not flower and fruit for several years because they are concentrating their energy on vegetative growth, in particular the struggle to reach the forest canopy and the essential light it gives. All trees must flower eventually in order to reproduce themselves. As trees vary considerably, so do the flowers they produce. Some, such as cherries (Prunus) and crab apples (Malus) produce showy flowers, not for our benefit, but to attract pollinating insects. Many trees, however are wind pollinated, and often (as in oaks, birches and hornbeams), have separate male and female catkins.

Successful pollination leads to the development of the fruit. This is equally varied, ranging from the fleshy red fruits of hawthorns and rowans, to the winged 'helicopters' of maples and the pods of the Judas tree. All fruits, no matter how different, share one feature. They all contain the seeds of the next generation.

TREE INTRODUCTIONS

In gardens we can bring together trees from around the world and species which would never normally meet are grown together. Today it seems perfectly natural to find a Chinese maple growing close to a North American oak. Of course, this has not always been the case and although several trees were probably distributed by the Romans, mainly for culinary purposes, it is only in the last three or four hundred years that trees have seriously been collected for ornament. Trees now common in gardens in the UK, for example, came from the species-rich forests of the eastern United States during the

17th and 18th centuries while the western states yielded their riches when visited by David Douglas in the early 19th century, and later by John Jeffrey. Collections came from Chile in the early 19th century when William Lobb was sent by the Veitch nursery, with additional introductions made by Richard Pierce and Harold Comber. The first collections in Japan were made by Philipp von Siebold in the early 19th century, with later visits by Charles Sargent and Charles Maries.

China was the country that proved to be the richest source of plants for temperate gardens. The first important introductions from there came from French missionaries, Armand David, Jean Delavay and Paul Farges in the late 19th century. Later many collectors explored China's wealth such as Reginald Farrer, Frank Kingdon-Ward, Joseph Rock, George Forrest, and perhaps the most prolific of all collectors, Ernest Wilson.

TREES IN GARDENS

While tree species can show considerable variation in the wild, they will often show much more when brought into cultivation. While unusual forms, such as those with variegated, purple, or yellow foliage, can certainly occur in natural populations, they are often weaker growing and as they have to compete with more vigorous seedlings, they may not survive very long. In cultivation, however, they can be selected and carefully nurtured under ideal conditions. They can then be propagated in a way that retains their unusual characteristic. These forms are known as cultivars, because, in effect, they are cultivated varieties. Cultivars make up a large proportion of garden trees. The upright growing *Prunus 'Amanogawa'*, for example, is one as are the numerous garden forms of the Lawson cypress, *Chamaecyparis lawsoniana*.

If trees are raised from garden seed they can produce hybrids with other species growing close to them. Hybrids can occur in natural populations but often when two species grow together in the wild there are natural barriers to them crossing with each other. In other cases species grow in gardens may never meet in the wild, and will never have developed natural barriers to prevent hybridisation. While this can cause confusion of the identity of some cultivated plants it can also give rise to new ones.

A good example of this is the red horse chestnut, *Aesculus × carnea*. This tree is in fact a hybrid between the common horse chestnut, *Aesculus hippocastanum*, a native of northern Greece and Albania, and the North American red buckeye, *A. pavia*. Believed to have been originated in the early 19th century, the red horse chestnut is a hybrid which could never naturally occur in the wild.

For many of us a tree is our most familiar symbol of the natural world. It represents freedom, a chance to escape from our increasingly hostile environment. Whatever our underlying reasons, we all benefit from the therapeutic influence of trees, whether we simply enjoy the dappled calm of a forest glade or rejoice in the life and colour that a single tree can bring to a bleak city street. It is only logical, therefore, that this identification with trees leads us to become curious about the types of species that grow near to us, so that enjoyment and study become one pursuit. It is to foster and maintain this pursuit that this book has been prepared.

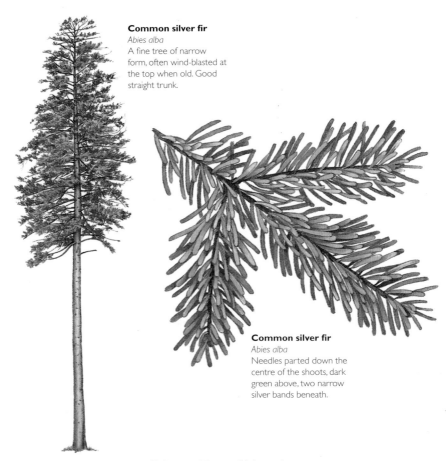

Common silver fir
Abies alba
A fine tree of narrow form, often wind-blasted at the top when old. Good straight trunk.

Common silver fir
Abies alba
Needles parted down the centre of the shoots, dark green above, two narrow silver bands beneath.

Silver Firs *(Abies)*

With about 50 species, all evergreen, the silver firs are one of the largest groups of conifers, widely distributed within the northern hemisphere, native to Europe, Asia, the Himalayas, North America and North Africa, and much used in forestry. The characteristic general features of silver firs are as follows: upright cones that break up while still on the tree; short, leathery, usually flattish needles set singly, leaving circular scars when they fall, and if pulled off the shoots they do not tear away or splinter as occurs with the spruces (*Picea*). Most species have silver stomata lines on the lower surface of the needles, hence the name 'silver' firs. They have persistent vertical leading shoots resulting in very straight trunks, and in many species the young bark is beset with resin blisters.

Common silver fir
(Abies alba syn. *A. pectinata)*
Native to the mountains of central and southern Europe, the common silver fir is a major tree in the forestry of these regions, growing up to 55m (180ft) and yielding large volumes of whitish, soft, straight-grained timber with a very wide range of uses. Unfortunately it does not succeed well in Britain or America owing

Pacific silver fir
Abies amabilis
Another fine tree of very regular conic form with dense foliage and lower branches downswept, often touching the ground.

Pacific silver fir
Abies amabilis
Typical mature foliage, dark, glossy green above, two silver bands below. New needles are glaucous all over.

to severe aphid attacks. Its needles, 1–2.5cm (½–1in) long, are shallowly notched at the tip, arranged in two opposite sets, parted down the middle, dark green above, with narrow white bands below. The cones, 10–15cm (4–6in), have down-turned, pointed bracts.

Pacific silver fir or red fir
(Abies amabilis)
The Latin 'amabilis' means 'lovely fir' and it is indeed a beautiful tree, reaching 75m (250ft) in its native stands along the west coast of British Columbia and in the Cascade mountains. It has curved, spreading needles, up to 3cm (1¼in) long,

glaucous-green at first, dark glossy green later, with two silver bands on the under surface and an orangy scent when crushed. The cones, 10–15cm (4–6in) long, are dark purple at first, brown later.

Balsam fir *(Abies balsamea)*
A small tree, seldom more than 22m (76ft) high, this has a wide native range, especially in Canada and northeastern USA. It is mainly known for the production of Canadian balsam from its resin blisters, and for its dwarf cultivar, 'Hudsonia', only about 50cm to 1m (20in–3ft) high, with very densely crowded small branches.

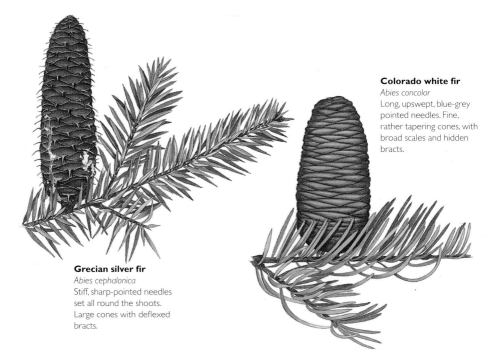

Colorado white fir
Abies concolor
Long, upswept, blue-grey
pointed needles. Fine,
rather tapering cones, with
broad scales and hidden
bracts.

Grecian silver fir
Abies cephalonica
Stiff, sharp-pointed needles
set all round the shoots.
Large cones with deflexed
bracts.

Nikko fir
(Abies brachyphylla syn. *A. homolepis)*
Common in the mountains of central
Japan, Nikko fir is a good ornamental
tree because its needles tend to grow
rather vertically, thus displaying their
bright silver bands on the lower surfaces.

Santa Lucia fir
(Abies bracteata syn. *A. venusta)*
A large tree, up to 45m (150ft) in California, this has distinctive, very long,
sharply pointed needles, up to 5cm (2in)
long, dark green above with bright silver
bands below and very long (up to
5cm/2in) protruding bracts to its cones,
which are 8–12cm (3–5in) high.

Greek fir *(Abies cephalonica)*
This mountain tree of Greece grows up
to 32m (105ft) tall, and is distinguished
by its sharp pointed needles, 2–3cm
(¾–1¼in) long, and radiating all round
the shoot, the upper surface shining
green, the lower side with two silver

bands. The cones are up to 15 x 5cm (6 x
2in), but the protruding bracts are
smaller than in Caucasian silver fir
(Abies nordmanniana).

Colorado white fir *(Abies concolor)*
A forest tree in western USA and parts of
Mexico, up to 60m (200ft) tall. It has
long needles, up to 5cm (2in), blue-grey
on both surfaces, all upswept, and many
cultivars have especially blue or silver
foliage. The cones are smooth, up to 15 x
4cm (6 x 1½in), green then light brown.

Delavay's silver fir *(Abies delavayi)*
Common in south-west China, where it
grows to 30m (100ft) tall, *Abies delavayi*
and its varieties *georgii, forrestii, fabri*
and *faxoniana* are grown as ornamental
trees loved for their dark shining green
needles with bright silver bands on the
underside, and their striking purple-blue
cones, up to 12 x 5cm (5 x 2in), with
finely pointed, small, exserted bracts.
Fairly young trees bear cones.

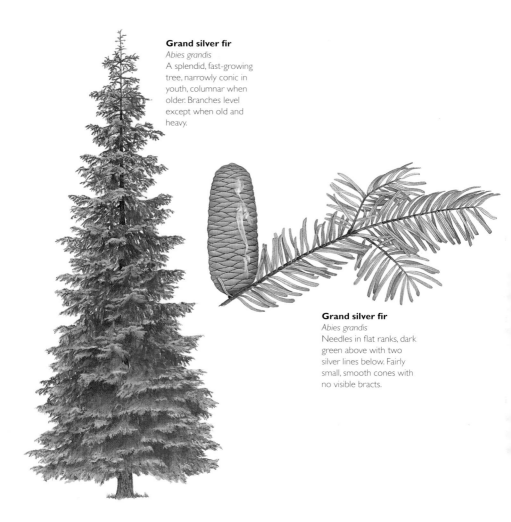

Grand silver fir
Abies grandis
A splendid, fast-growing tree, narrowly conic in youth, columnar when older. Branches level except when old and heavy.

Grand silver fir
Abies grandis
Needles in flat ranks, dark green above with two silver lines below. Fairly small, smooth cones with no visible bracts.

Grand or giant silver fir *(Abies grandis)*
This splendid species from Vancouver Island to the interior of southern British Columbia and south to California is of extraordinary vigour and speed of growth; as a result, it is very popular for forestry. Native trees have reached a height of 90m (300ft), and in Britain it is already the tallest tree, having topped 55m (180ft) although only introduced in 1832. The flat leaves, 2–5cm (¾–2in) long x 3mm (⅛in) wide, are dark shiny green above with two silvery bands below; they are arranged horizontally in an almost flat layer, with shorter needles uppermost. They have a slight notch at the tip and are very aromatic when bruised. The small blunt buds are dark purple, unless covered with white resin. Flowers occur only in the upper crown of mature trees; the males are purplish and 3mm (⅛in) across, the females upright, 1.5cm (⅝in) tall, green and purplish. The cones are up to 9 x 4cm (3½ x 1½in), green at first, reddish brown when ripe; they often have white resin spots. Young bark has resin blisters, old bark is dark grey, cracking into small irregular plates.

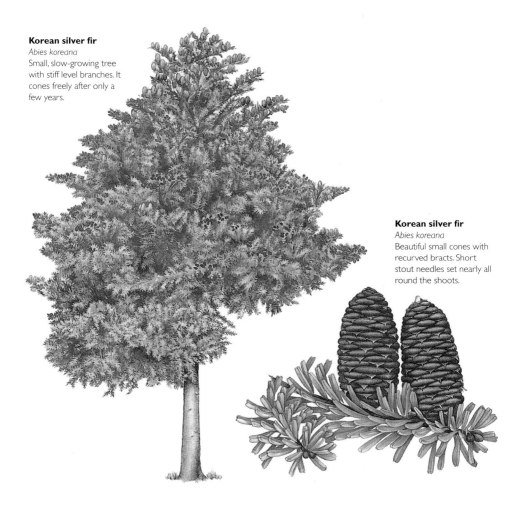

Korean silver fir
Abies koreana
Small, slow-growing tree with stiff level branches. It cones freely after only a few years.

Korean silver fir
Abies koreana
Beautiful small cones with recurved bracts. Short stout needles set nearly all round the shoots.

Korean fir *(Abies koreana)*

From the mountains of Quelpaert Island, this remarkable slow-growing little tree cones freely when only just over 1m (3ft) high and is of broad, stiff, conic form with short, blunt, notched needles radiating round the shoot, glossy green above with bright white stomata bands beneath. It is a charming little tree, especially when flowering, the male flowers opening in bright yellow clusters and the upright females 2–4cm (¾–1½in) tall and light purple. The cones are small, 4–7cm (1½–3in) high, deep blue at first, brown later with recurved exserted bracts.

Alpine fir *(Abies lasiocarpa)*

This species has the widest distribution of any North American fir, from Alaska to New Mexico. On good sites it will reach 40m (130ft) and it is of beautiful slender, spire-like form, with dense blue-green foliage. The cones are 11–15cm (4½–6in), barrel-shaped with pubescent scales, brown when ripe. The variety *arizonica* (cork fir) has thick, soft bark.

California red fir *(Abies magnifica)*

Another species from California, Oregon and Sierra Nevada, it is very like noble silver fir (*Abies procera*) except for the following points: *A. magnifica* is not so

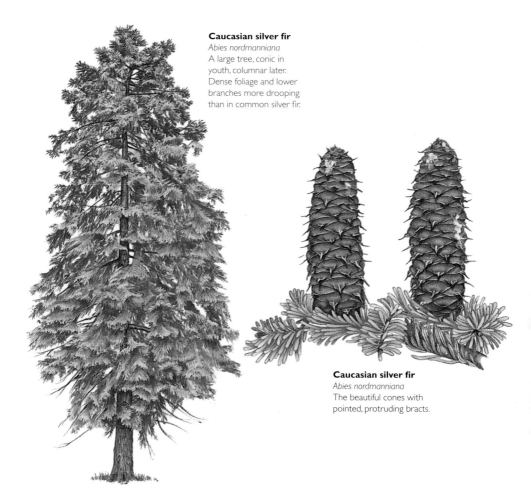

Caucasian silver fir
Abies nordmanniana
A large tree, conic in youth, columnar later. Dense foliage and lower branches more drooping than in common silver fir.

Caucasian silver fir
Abies nordmanniana
The beautiful cones with pointed, protruding bracts.

large and is of narrower conic form; the bark is red-brown on old trees; the needles, longer and less densely set, are more rounded in section; the cones are a little shorter and wider, with more down on the scales and the bracts less flattened to the cone.

Caucasian silver fir
(Abies nordmanniana)

Another giant, this time from the western Caucasus and north-east Turkey, soaring to 70m (230ft) in height with fine, lustrous dark green foliage; it makes a splendid ornamental tree. The needles are dense, pointing forwards, with bright silver bands beneath and no parting on the upper side of the twig. The cones are up to 15 x 5cm (6 x 2in), with protruding bracts bent down.

Spanish or hedgehog fir *(Abies pinsapo)*
Like Greek fir (*A. cephalonica*), the needles of this tree, from southern Spain, radiate all round the shoot; however, they are shorter, approximately 1.5cm (½in) thicker, stiffer, grey-blue all round, and on older twigs tend to curve backwards. The cones are smaller, up to 10cm (4in) long, with no protruding bracts. Spanish fir is unique in appearance, and makes an attractive ornamental tree.

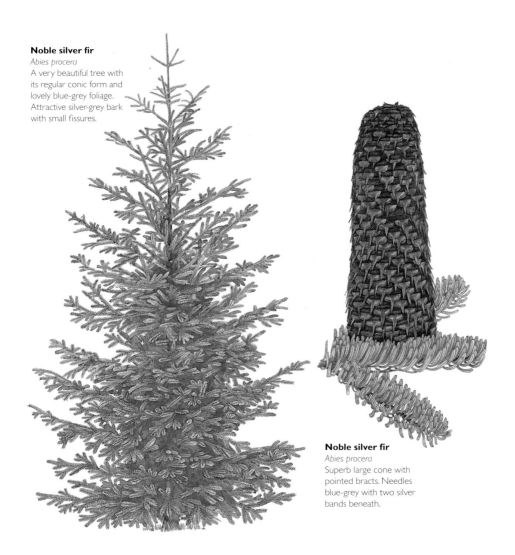

Noble silver fir
Abies procera
A very beautiful tree with its regular conic form and lovely blue-grey foliage. Attractive silver-grey bark with small fissures.

Noble silver fir
Abies procera
Superb large cone with pointed bracts. Needles blue-grey with two silver bands beneath.

Noble silver fir

(Abies procera syn. A. nobilis)

From Washington to northern California and northwest Oregon, this is another magnificent tree reaching to 80m (260ft) and living up to 700 years, although it is not as fast-growing as the grand or giant silver fir (*A. grandis*). The small buds are hidden by little needles crowding all over the upper side of the twigs, pointing forwards and upwards, and parted into two ranks on the lower side. Normal needles are bluish grey-green on both surfaces, bent at the base, with no notch at the tip. They are very different from *A. grandis* needles. The bright crimson male flowers are globular, 5mm (¼in) across and crowded on the underside of the twigs; the females are upright, about 3cm (1¼in) tall, and yellowish green. The cones, green and purple at first, turning brown later, are the finest of all the silver firs. Measuring 18–25cm (7–10in) tall x 7–9cm (3–3½in) wide, with attractive spi-

Veitch's silver fir
Abies veitchii
Beautiful silver-backed
needles with blunt ends
and fairly small cones,
often resinous, with only
the tops of the bracts
showing.

rally arranged protruding bracts bent
over against the scales, they are usually
erect, but sometimes bent over by their
own weight. The beautiful mature bark is
silvery grey with fine fissures; young bark
is marked with resin blisters. Noble silver
fir is a very handsome ornamental tree.

Himalayan fir *(Abies spectabilis* syn. *A.
webbiana* and very close to *A. pindrow)*
This tree is valued for its superb dark
green foliage with brilliant silver bands
on the underside and for the large grey-
blue cones, up to 18 x 7cm (7 x 3in). In
its native Himalayan home it grows to
60m (200ft) tall.

Veitch's silver fir *(Abies veitchii)*
A medium-sized ornamental tree, up to
22m (76ft) tall, this comes from the
mountains of central Spain. Its attractive
and unusual needles are truncated, being
cut off at their broadest point, tapering
towards the base, dark glossy green
above, with broad silver bands below,
densely set on the top of the shoots and
pointing forwards and upwards. Cones
appear on fairly young trees and are
6–8cm (2½–3in) tall, with smoothly wrinkled scales and the tips of the bracts only
just visible.

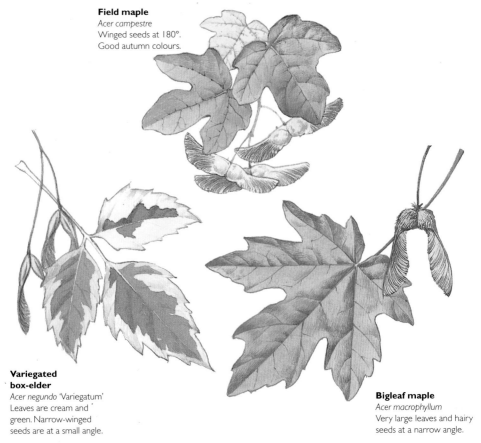

Field maple
Acer campestre
Winged seeds at 180°.
Good autumn colours.

Variegated box-elder
Acer negundo 'Variegatum'
Leaves are cream and
green. Narrow-winged
seeds are at a small angle.

Bigleaf maple
Acer macrophyllum
Very large leaves and hairy
seeds at a narrow angle.

Maples (Acer)

This large and important genus consists of about 150 species in north temperate regions. It provides some of our finest ornamental trees, their special feature being marvellous autumn colours; these are seen on the grandest scale in North America but, owing to the increasing use of the beautiful Japanese varieties, are now more widespread.

The majority of maples have the following general characteristics: seeds in pairs, joined at the base, each with a one-sided membranous wing; opposite leaves, usually lobed or pinnate but a few are entire and nearly all are deciduous.

Field maple (Acer campestre)
This is the common hedgerow maple of Europe and western Asia, often scrubby when cut back but when allowed to grow freely it makes a beautiful tree up to 25m (80ft) tall. The small leaves, 5–10cm (2–4in) across, have three main lobes and two small basal ones; they are usually broader than long and grow on slender stalks; in spring, they are a pretty reddish colour, turning to gold in autumn. The yellow, red and green horizontally opposed winged seeds are also decorative. The older twigs often have narrow corky wings.

Red snake-bark maple *(Acer capillipes)*
This Japanese tree, up to 15m (50ft) tall, has green bark with white stripes and a very upright form. The leaves, approximately 9 x 12cm (3½ x 5in), have large, pointed central lobes and two small side lobes, and turn to shades of red and yellow-orange in autumn.

David's maple *(Acer davidii)*
Another Chinese species, this is very variable and some botanists divide it into several species. It grows up to 18m (60ft) tall, the lower branches being level, the upper ones ascending and arching over; the bark is olive-green, with broad silver stripes. The leaves (not all maple-like) are simple and ovate, with a pointed end, unevenly toothed, dark shiny green above and whitish green on the underside at the start of the season, turning to bright yellow, orange or red in autumn.

Paperbark maple *(Acer griseum)*
This small tree, seldom above 13m (43ft) tall, has wonderful coppery brown, shiny, peeling bark on both trunk and branches, making a beautiful contrast with the tri-foliate leaves, which are dark grey-green above and bluish white beneath. A native of western China, it is one of the best of the ornamentals and gives good red autumn colour. The greenish yellow flowers hang in little bunches of three to five on long stalks, and the fat seeds have almost parallel broad wings.

Downy Japanese maple
(Acer japonicum)
A small broad-crowned tree, this grows to 10m (30ft) tall, with a short bole quickly dividing into many sinuous branches, with greyish bark. The light green, almost circular leaves, about 7–12cm (3–5in) in diameter, with 7 to 11 lobes cut not more than two-fifths towards the leaf base, have irregular small-toothed edges and silky hairs all over when just opened, both on leaves and stalks. Later they are only retained on the underside of the leaf veins. The small purple flowers, about 1cm (½in) across, form in long-stalked nodding bunches; winged seed pairs, almost horizontally spread, are greenish on red stalks. Autumn colours are usually good, mainly reds with some golds, but less brilliant than with many of its cultivars.

'Vitifolium' is very similar but tends to be larger. The leaves are also bigger, and are usually 9- to 12-lobed; the autumn colours are more brilliant. 'Filicifolium', syn. 'Aconitifolium', has more deeply divided and serrated leaves that turn a very rich ruby colour in autumn.

Bigleaf or Oregon maple
(Acer macrophyllum)
This is the only commercially important maple of the Pacific Coast region, with a native range from Alaska to California. It grows to 30m (100ft) and forms a tall-domed crown of ascending branches. It is notable for its very large three- to five-lobed leaves, usually wider than long, 18–30cm x 20–35cm (7–12in x 8–14in), glossy green above, paler beneath, on green or red stalks, 15–25cm (6–10in) long. The scented flowers hang in narrow racemes, 12–20cm (5–8in) long.

Box-elder or ash-leafed maple
(Acer negundo)
An eastern North American species, this seldom grows above 20m (70ft). Each of the long-stalked pinnate leaves has five to seven leaflets, much like those of ash *(Fraxinus)* or elder *(Sambucus)*; their autumn colours are not remarkable. The pairs of narrow-winged seeds are bent inwards so that the wings are parallel.

The cultivar 'Variegatum' has leaves variegated with pure white and is more

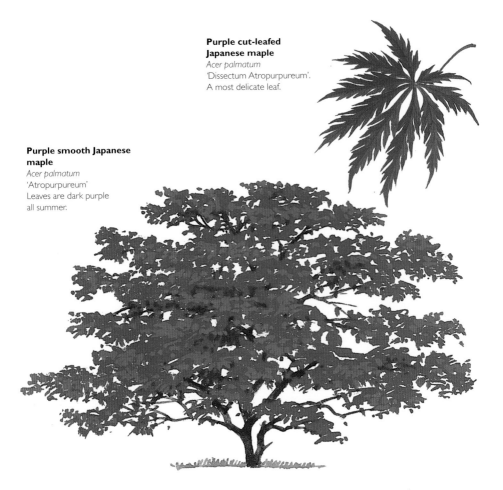

Purple cut-leafed Japanese maple
Acer palmatum
'Dissectum Atropurpureum'.
A most delicate leaf.

Purple smooth Japanese maple
Acer palmatum
'Atropurpureum'
Leaves are dark purple all summer.

often planted than the original green type, but it tends to revert to green with sucker growths from the base.

Smooth Japanese maple

(Acer palmatum)

This grows up to 15m (50ft) tall and is often less broad than downy Japanese maple (*Acer japonicum*), with the sinuous branches a little more ascending before they arch down; the bark tends to be browner. The green leaves have five to seven pointed lobes cut halfway or more towards the base, finely serrated edges and no pubescence. Purple flowers, about 7mm (¼in) across, grow in erect small panicles; the pale red winged seeds are in little bunches, with the pairs of wings set at 80 or 90°. Autumn colours are bronze or purple.

The cultivar 'Atropurpureum' has rich purple leaves throughout the summer, in some trees bronze, in others more red. 'Aureum' has light yellow leaves, which turn deep gold in autumn. 'Dissectum' has very deeply cut green leaves, and 'Dissectum Atropurpureum' has very deeply cut purple leaves.

'Osakazuki' is one of the best of all the cultivars. The leaves usually have seven long acuminate lobes and start as soft green in colour, often tinged with bronze or pink round the edges, turning to bril-

Striped maple
Acer pensylvanicum
Broad three-lobed leaves
are sharply serrated.
Curved seed-wings form a
crescent.

Norway maple
Acer platanoides
Seeds at a wide
angle. Lovely leaves.

liant scarlet in autumn; during the summer the bright red winged seeds contrast well with the green foliage.

'Senkaki', the coral bark maple, has coral red bark on the twigs and smaller branches, and small, deeply cut yellow-green leaves.

Striped maple or moose-bark
(*Acer pensylvanicum*)

This tree from eastern Canada and northeastern USA grows up to 12m (40ft) tall, with very erect branches and grey-green bark brilliantly striped with white lines. The large, three-pointed leaves, up to 13 x 22cm (5 x 9in), turn clear yellow in autumn.

Norway maple (*Acer platanoides*)

A Scandinavian and North European tree, similar to but less hardy in Britain than sycamore (*Acer pseudoplatanus*), *A. platanoides* grows up to 30m (100ft) tall. It has an ascending branch habit, tall-domed crown and often a short bole. One of its special features is the bright greenish yellow flowers in erect bunches of 20 to 40, which come out before the leaves and make a beautiful sight in early spring. The leaf buds are more pointed than those of sycamore, and are red-brown; the thin-textured leaves have lobes ending in fine points and turn to brilliant colours in autumn, often mixed

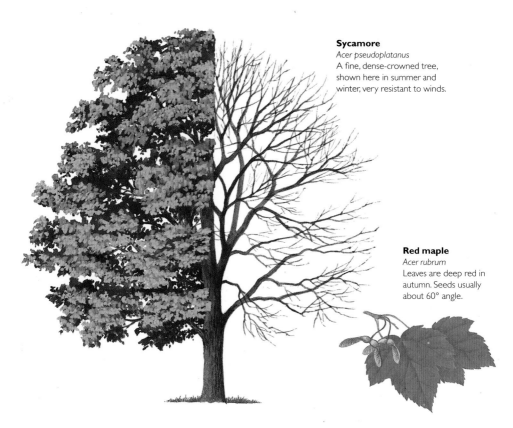

Sycamore
Acer pseudoplatanus
A fine, dense-crowned tree,
shown here in summer and
winter, very resistant to winds.

Red maple
Acer rubrum
Leaves are deep red in
autumn. Seeds usually
about 60° angle.

gold, red and green, but eventually gold dominates. The winged seeds are set at an angle of 140–180°. The bark fissures into fine ridges. 'Crimson King' is a good cultivar, with crimson leaves redder than most of the several purple varieties.

Sycamore *(Acer pseudoplatanus)*
This splendid, very hardy tree grows to 35m (120ft) tall with a large, broad, domed crown and girths up to 7m (22ft). Native and common over large areas in central and southern Europe, it was probably introduced by the Romans into Britain, where it thrives even on exposed hill country. It has ovoid greenish buds, and the large leaves, up to 18 x 24cm (7 x 10in), usually wider than long, on 6–12cm (2½–5in) stalks, commonly have five coarsely and unevenly toothed lobes, often reddish in colour. The flowers hang

in yellow-green tassels, 6–12cm (2½–5in) long, followed by bunches of winged seeds, green at first and later tinged with red, each pair being set at an angle of 70–120°. The bark on young trees is smooth, but in older trees it flakes off in squarish scales, often curled at the edge to expose pinkish fawn patches.

Two interesting cultivars of sycamore are 'Brilliantissimum', whose leaves emerge pink then turn light yellow, and are very conspicuous until late summer, when they turn green, and 'Purpureum', with beautiful purple leaves.

Red maple *(Acer rubrum)*
Red maple has much the same native distribution as sugar maple (*A. saccharum*), and the two often grow together. The red maple is a smaller tree, rarely above 30m (100ft). Its smaller, narrower leaves have

Sugar maple
Acer saccharum
Thin three- to five-lobed leaves. Winged seeds at medium angle.

Red maple
Acer rubrum
A fine, narrow-crowned tree, shown here in summer.

Sugar maple
Acer saccharum
Irregular-domed crown. Red-gold in autumn.

more forward-pointing lobes and more little teeth round the edges. It usually offers marvellous autumn colours in bright reds.

Sugar maple *(Acer saccharum)*
Sugar maple is one of the major species responsible for the magnificent autumn colours in North America. It grows to 35m (120ft) tall, with an irregular-domed crown, and its thin-textured leaf, up to 12 x 18cm (5 x 7in), has three to five pointed lobes and a stalk 3–7cm (1¼–3in) long. Sugar maple is one of the largest and most important hardwoods in the eastern half of the USA. It is a valuable timber tree, and is also the source of maple sugar and maple syrup, obtained by tapping the sap in spring. The sugar maple leaf in autumn is the national emblem of Canada.

Red horse chestnut
Aesculus × carnea
Shown here in spring, this
is much less vigorous than
the white form, with
smaller leaves and nuts.

Red horse chestnut
Aesculus × carnea
Short pinkish red flower
spikes, and darker,
rougher leaves than in
white horse chestnut.

Horse Chestnuts (Aesculus)

Most of this group of over 20 species originate from America, where they are called 'buckeyes' because the pale patch on the base of the dark nuts resembles the eye of a deer. However, some horse chestnuts are from southern Europe, China, Japan and the Himalayas. They all have large digitate leaves, erect panicles of flowers and big nuts.

Red horse chestnut
(Aesculus × carnea)

With its attractive dark pink flowers in spikes reaching up to 20cm (8in) tall, this hybrid between *Aesculus hippocastanum* and *A. pavia* is much smaller and slower growing than its white-flowered parent and very subject to stem cankers. Its nuts are also smaller, and the husks have many fewer prickles.

Sweet or yellow buckeye
(Aesculus flava syn. A. octandra)

Of the several American species, this is the most vigorous, growing up to 32m (105ft), with twisting branches, yellow flowers in spikes up to 18cm (7in) high, smooth nut-husks and smooth, reddish brown bark flaking in small scales.

Horse chestnut
(Aesculus hippocastanum)

This is one of the finest of all the

Sweet or yellow buckeye
Aesculus flava
Smaller, shinier leaves than horse chestnut. Orange-red autumn colours. Nut husks without spines.

Horse chestnut
Aesculus hippocastanum
Leaflets are usually in fives. Rich glossy brown nuts.

broadleaved trees, presenting a wonderful sight all through the year. It is of grand stature, up to 40m (130ft) tall, and has a huge domed crown and great spreading lower branches that bend downwards and then sweep up sharply towards the tips. Native to Albania and northern Greece, but now spread widely through Europe, North America, and many other countries, horse chestnut is a favourite tree for parks and large gardens. It is loved for its large shining brown buds, sticky in spring and opening quickly; magnificent in late spring, when covered with its large, upright spikes of white flowers, up to 26cm (10in) tall, each with little patches of yellow or pink; and glorious in its rich autumn gold and abundant crop of large, rich brown, beautifully marked nuts or 'conkers' in their prickly, globular, green husks.

Each large leaf has from five to seven finely toothed leaflets, radiating from a fairly long stalk, the centre leaflet may be as large as 22 x 10cm (9 x 4in) and broadest towards the tip. The leaf scars are large and marked like little horseshoes; but the name 'horse' chestnut probably comes from Turkey, where the nuts were fed to horses and alleged to

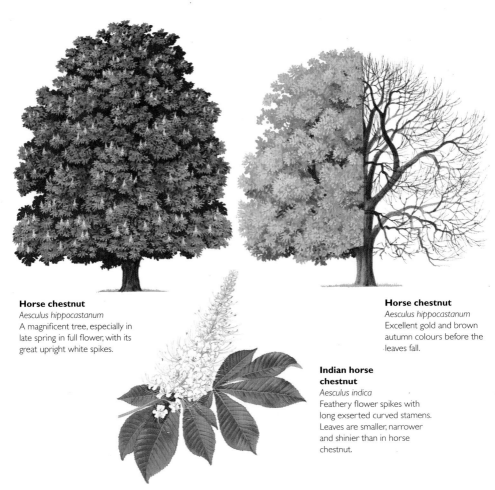

Horse chestnut
Aesculus hippocastanum
A magnificent tree, especially in
late spring in full flower, with its
great upright white spikes.

Horse chestnut
Aesculus hippocastanum
Excellent gold and brown
autumn colours before the
leaves fall.

**Indian horse
chestnut**
Aesculus indica
Feathery flower spikes with
long exserted curved stamens.
Leaves are smaller, narrower
and shinier than in horse
chestnut.

cure broken wind. Old trunks are often
spirally fluted, and the bark breaks away
in irregular plates and scales.

Indian horse chestnut *(Aesculus indica)*
From the Himalayas, this tree reaches
30m (100ft) in India but seldom more
than 20m (70ft) elsewhere. It is a graceful tree with smaller, more shiny leaves
than most chestnuts and very attractive
feathery flower spikes up to 30cm (12in)
tall. These are mainly white but have red
and yellow blotches and projecting thin
stamens that give a 'bottle brush' effect.

Red buckeye *(Aesculus pavia)*
This species seldom reaches above 12m

(40ft); its flowers are darker red than
those of *Aesculus* × *carnea*. Another
hybrid, *A.* × *planteriensis*, is a much
more vigorous tree, reaching 25m (80ft),
with larger pale pink flower spikes.

Dwarf buckeye or shrubby pavia
(Aesculus parviflora)
This species, originating from southeastern USA, is scarcely a tree, since it is
seldom more than 4m (12ft) high and
usually has a crowd of small stems from
sucker growth. It is hardy and has beautiful white flower spikes, 20–32cm
(8–13in) high, with lovely pinkish white,
thread-like stamens.

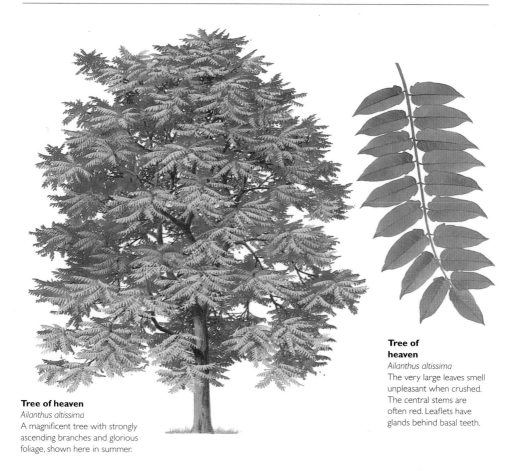

Tree of heaven
Ailanthus altissima
A magnificent tree with strongly
ascending branches and glorious
foliage, shown here in summer.

Tree of heaven
Ailanthus altissima
The very large leaves smell
unpleasant when crushed.
The central stems are
often red. Leaflets have
glands behind basal teeth.

Tree of Heaven *(Ailanthus altissima)*

Native to China, the tree of heaven was introduced to Europe, America and various subtropical countries in the eighteenth century. It is a good example of an impressive tree cultivated mainly for its lovely, exotic-looking foliage. Other benefits are that it grows vigorously and tolerates pollution.

The leaves are huge and compound, and may reach a length of 60cm (24in) on normal trees, or a full metre (3ft) on coppiced shoots. Each leaf resembles a branch; it has up to 50 small side leaflets, plus a solitary one at its tip. When the leaves open very late in spring, they are bronze in colour. They soon turn dark green, and break up in autumn without changing colour.

The flowers open in midsummer, in large, loose panicles of tiny white blossoms, all of one sex, though both sexes can occur on one tree. They have an acrid odour. Each blossom may be male, with ten stamens bearing yellow anthers, or female, with a central pistil. They soon fade and the tree then attracts little attention until early autumn, when the large seed-wings turn from green to gold and the centre of each wing, holding one seed, turns rich orange-crimson.

Italian alder
Alnus cordata
The lovely catkins and red female flowers.

Italian alder
Alnus cordata
Glossy, quite differently shaped leaves and larger seed pods.

Common alder
Alnus glutinosa
Mature leaves and young next year's catkins (which turn purple by mid-autumn).

Common alder
Alnus glutinosa
The curiously cone-like seed vessels remain empty on the tree for a long time.

Alders (*Alnus*)

A genus of about 30 species growing mainly in the northern hemisphere, alders are associated with streamsides and other wet sites. The buds form on short stalks and the rounded leaves are alternate; the fruit is small, woody and ovoid, cone-like in structure and very persistent on the twigs. Nodules caused by nitrogen-fixing bacteria, *Schinzia alni*, form on the roots. Several species tend to throw up suckers from the roots.

Italian alder (*Alnus cordata*)
Native to Corsica and southern Italy, this is the most handsome of all the alders, growing to 27m (90ft) tall, with beautiful shining green leaves, fine pink and gold male catkins and bright crimson little female flowers. It will grow on drier sites than common alder (*Alnus glutinosa*).

Common or black alder
(*Alnus glutinosa*)
Native throughout Europe and North Africa, this attractive streamside tree grows to about 27m (90ft) tall, with ascending branches and a usually narrow form. It has purplish buds on short stalks, broad leaves, up to 7 x 10cm (3 x 4in), with a rounded apex and wavy, shallow-toothed margins.

The male catkins, 6–12cm (2½–5in),

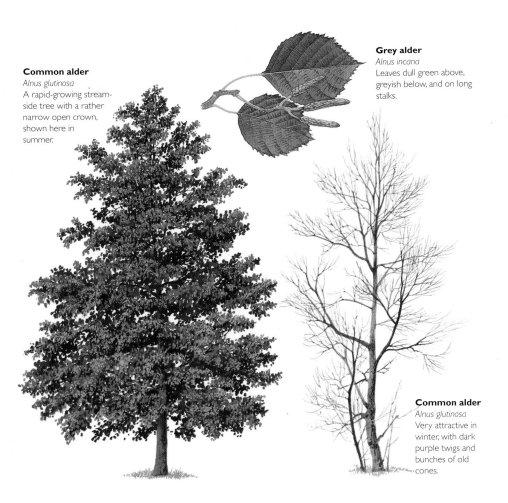

Grey alder
Alnus incana
Leaves dull green above, greyish below, and on long stalks.

Common alder
Alnus glutinosa
A rapid-growing stream-side tree with a rather narrow open crown, shown here in summer.

Common alder
Alnus glutinosa
Very attractive in winter, with dark purple twigs and bunches of old cones.

several together, are purple in winter, turning yellow tinged crimson when ripe; the female flowers are dark red, up to 6mm (¼in) long, in short, erect small clusters; seeds form in a hard woody cone, 10–18mm (½–¾in) long. The grey-brown bark is shallowly fissured on older trees.

Grey alder *(Alnus incana)*
Native to Europe, the Caucasus and eastern North America, this is a hardy species, tolerating colder sites than most alders. Its leaves are distinct: ovate, coarsely toothed, dull green above, greyish beneath, often with pubescent surfaces, either pointed or rounded.

Himalayan alder *(Alnus nitida)*
This fine alder, up to 35m (120ft) tall, has ovate leaves, 8–16cm (3–6in) long, and flowers in the autumn. The male catkins are up to 16cm (6in) and the fruits are erect, 2–4cm (¾–1½in) long.

Red or Oregon alder
(Alnus rubra syn. *A. oregona)*
The red or Oregon alder is common right down the west coast of North America from Alaska to California. The buds usually tend to be red, though on some trees they may be mostly green, and the ovate, bluntly pointed leaves have finely toothed edges.

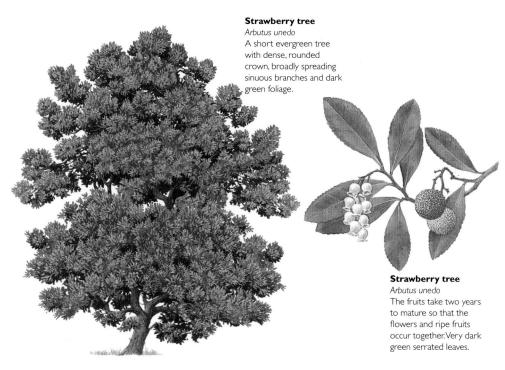

Strawberry tree
Arbutus unedo
A short evergreen tree
with dense, rounded
crown, broadly spreading
sinuous branches and dark
green foliage.

Strawberry tree
Arbutus unedo
The fruits take two years
to mature so that the
flowers and ripe fruits
occur together. Very dark
green serrated leaves.

Strawberry Trees (Arbutus)

This is a small group of about a dozen evergreen species belonging to the great Ericaceae or heather family. The fruits resemble small round strawberries, but are insipid-tasting.

Cyprus strawberry tree
(Arbutus andrachne)

This is very similar to *A. unedo* but its leaves are entire and smaller, its fruits smaller and smooth and it flowers in spring, not winter. Hybrids between these two species occur naturally in Greece (known as × *andrachnoides*); many are spectacular ornamental trees with beautiful orange-red peeling bark.

Madrona (Arbutus menziesii)

Commonly found wild from California to British Columbia, and conspicuous with its vivid orange-red bark, this magnificent tree reaches 30m (100ft) tall with oval, entire, leathery leaves, up to 12 x 7cm (5 x 3in), dark shining green above but a wonderful ice-blue beneath. The small white flowers appear in spring in upright panicles, and the fruits are only about 1cm (½in) across.

Strawberry tree (Arbutus unedo)

This small, rounded tree is native to the Mediterranean and parts of Ireland. It is 4–14m (12–46ft) tall, usually with a short bole quickly dividing into several crooked stems. The bark is reddish, later grey-brown with scales. The leathery, serrated, shiny, dark green leaves, up to 9 x 3cm (3½ x 1¼in), have pinkish green stalks. The ivory-coloured flowers, like little waxen bells, hang in bunches, opening from late autumn to mid-winter. The rough, pimply globose fruits, 2cm (¾in) in diameter, take two years to mature and are green at first, then yellow and finally bright red.

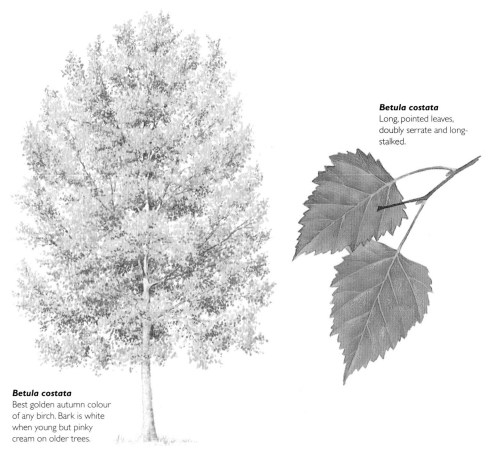

Betula costata
Long, pointed leaves,
doubly serrate and long-
stalked.

Betula costata
Best golden autumn colour
of any birch. Bark is white
when young but pinky
cream on older trees.

Birches *(Betula)*

There are over 40 species of this genus in Europe, Asia, the Himalayas and North America; some grow even within the Arctic Circle in Iceland, Greenland and Alaska. All have their flowers in catkins, the males drooping, the females upright; the seeds are small; and the leaves are alternate. The strikingly white bark, unusually tough and waterproof, is the dominant feature of many birches.

Betula costata

The special features of this handsome Asian birch are its very white bark and the wonderful deep gold colour of its leaves in autumn.

Erman's birch *(Betula ermanii)*
This native of Japan, Manchuria and northeast Asia grows to 30m (100ft) tall. It has broad, cylindrical catkins and leaves 6–9cm (2½–3½in) long. The bark is white in young trees, turning pinkish with horizontal stripes, and then shredding off later.

Cherry or sweet birch *(Betula lenta)*
This tree from the northeastern USA gets its name from its reddish brown bark, rather like that of a cherry; it is aromatic when young. The finely serrate leaves are edged with whisker-like points and turn orange and gold in autumn. In common

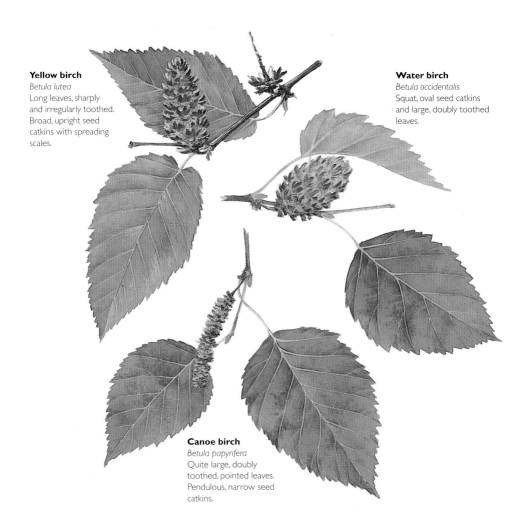

Yellow birch
Betula lutea
Long leaves, sharply and irregularly toothed. Broad, upright seed catkins with spreading scales.

Water birch
Betula occidentalis
Squat, oval seed catkins and large, doubly toothed leaves.

Canoe birch
Betula papyrifera
Quite large, doubly toothed, pointed leaves. Pendulous, narrow seed catkins.

with yellow birch (*Betula lutea*), the shoots are a source of oil of wintergreen.

Yellow birch
(Betula lutea syn. *B. alleghaniensis)*
This species from eastern North America grows to approximately 30m (100ft) tall. The shoots have a characteristic scent of oil of wintergreen when crushed. The leaves, 8–11cm x 4–6cm (3–4½in x 1½–2½in), pointed and doubly serrated, turn a bright yellow colour in autumn. The bark is silvery yellow, peeling to show golden-brown.

Japanese red birch or Maximowicz's birch
(Betula maximowicziana)
A fine, vigorous tree, up to 30m (100ft) tall, this has the largest leaves of any birch (8–14cm x 6–11cm/ 3–5½in x 2½–4½in), shaped like lime leaves. The male catkins grow to 9–14cm (3½–5½in), the females 3–7cm (1¼–3in), in racemes of two to four. The reddish bark becomes grey with age.

Dwarf birch *(Betula nana)*
This round-leaved bushy birch extends

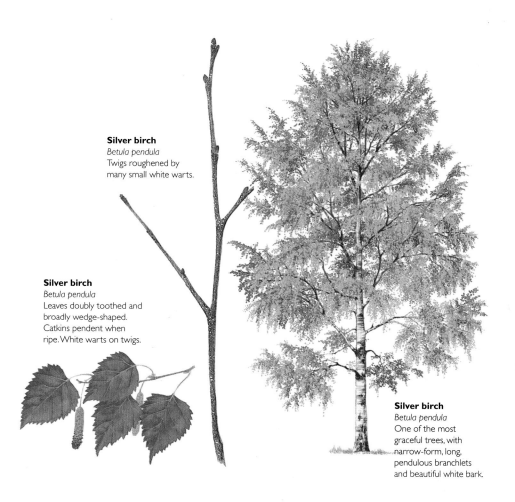

Silver birch
Betula pendula
Twigs roughened by
many small white warts.

Silver birch
Betula pendula
Leaves doubly toothed and
broadly wedge-shaped.
Catkins pendent when
ripe. White warts on twigs.

Silver birch
Betula pendula
One of the most
graceful trees, with
narrow-form, long,
pendulous branchlets
and beautiful white bark.

from northern Asia and Europe right up as far as the Arctic Circle in Greenland and to Alaska.

River birch (*Betula nigra*)

An eastern USA species growing to 30m (100ft) tall, river birch is distinguished by its bark — silvery brown at first, then dark blackish red-brown, flaking off in rolls and tatters from both trunk and branches. Its glossy green leaves have markedly double-serrate margins.

Water birch
(*Betula occidentalis* syn. *B. fontinalis*)

A native of the west coast of North Amer-ica from Canada to California, liking wet sites, this small, often bushy tree (5–10m/15–30ft) has broad, ovate, doubly serrate leaves, 2–5cm (¾–2in), and squat catkins.

Canoe or paper-bark birch
(*Betula papyrifera*)

This is the canoe birch of the Native Americans. It grows to 40m (130ft) tall and has smooth, peeling bark varying from cream to orange-pink, often strongly marked by horizontal bands; the leaves, 4–10cm (1½–4in), have stout hairy stalks.

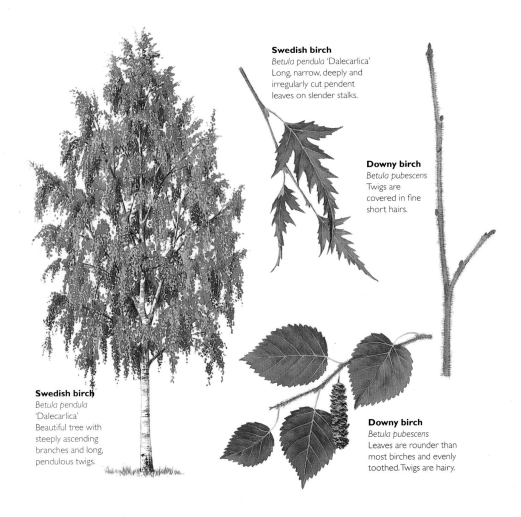

Swedish birch
Betula pendula 'Dalecarlica'
Long, narrow, deeply and
irregularly cut pendent
leaves on slender stalks.

Downy birch
Betula pubescens
Twigs are
covered in fine
short hairs.

Swedish birch
Betula pendula
'Dalecarlica'
Beautiful tree with
steeply ascending
branches and long,
pendulous twigs.

Downy birch
Betula pubescens
Leaves are rounder than
most birches and evenly
toothed. Twigs are hairy.

Silver birch

(Betula pendula syn. *B. verrucosa)*

Common in Europe and Asia, this species grows to 30m (100ft), having a narrow form, branches ascending when young but pendulous later, twigs with whitish warts, and doubly serrate pointed leaves. The white or pinkish white bark is often marked with black diamond-shaped ridges low on older trunks. In winter the twigs make a lovely purple haze against the sky.

'Dalecarlica', a Swedish cultivar of silver birch, has a narrow form, ascending branches, long pendulous twigs and deeply cut, long-pointed leaves. 'Youngii' (syn. 'Pendula') is a grafted, round-headed pendulous form.

Downy or white birch

(Betula pubescens)

Similar to the silver birch *(Betula pendula)* in size and distribution, the downy birch differs as follows: the branches are less pendulous and the twigs are hairy, not warty; the bark is whiter at middle age and without the black diamonds; the leaves are rounder, more evenly serrated, and on downy stalks.

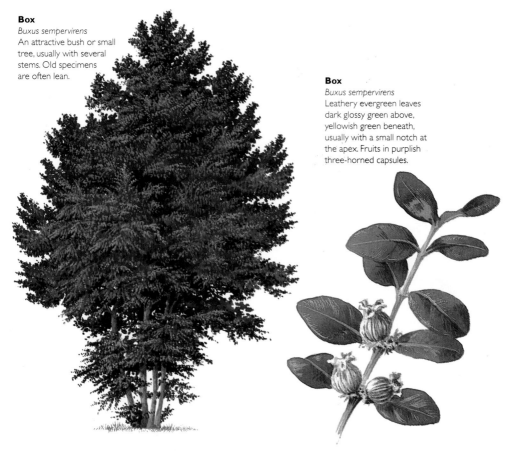

Box
Buxus sempervirens
An attractive bush or small tree, usually with several stems. Old specimens are often lean.

Box
Buxus sempervirens
Leathery evergreen leaves dark glossy green above, yellowish green beneath, usually with a small notch at the apex. Fruits in purplish three-horned capsules.

Box *(Buxus sempervirens)*

Box, like holly (*Ilex*), is one of the few evergreen broadleaved trees that thrive in northern Europe. It is limited to the western seaboard, where winters are comparatively mild, and suffers under the severer climates found further east; thus it flourishes on the fringe of a Mediterranean climate flora adapted to mild wet winters, followed by hot dry summers. As a result, it has thick, leathery leaves with waxy surfaces that slow down water loss through transpiration. It grows on chalk and limestone soils.

Box *(Buxus sempervirens)*
The leaves of box are set in pairs, and each has a neat oval shape, dark green above, paler below. The foliage is shade-tolerant, which enables close-ranked leaves to flourish beside one another. Hence the trees can be trained to form a dense hedge or be trained into shapes to resemble, for example, birds or castle battlements, by the art of tree sculpture known as topiary.

Its dwarf form, called 'Suffruticosa', is widely cultivated for low hedges throughout Europe and North America.

In late spring, box opens clusters of little yellow flowers set in leaf axils. Male flowers develop on the outer edges of

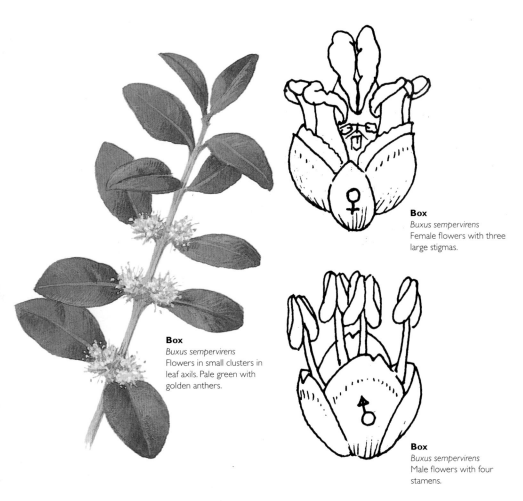

Box
Buxus sempervirens
Female flowers with three
large stigmas.

Box
Buxus sempervirens
Flowers in small clusters in
leaf axils. Pale green with
golden anthers.

Box
Buxus sempervirens
Male flowers with four
stamens.

each cluster, and female ones at its centre. All have four yellow sepals and four yellow petals. Male flowers bear four stamens with golden anthers, while female flowers have a single, flask-shaped, green pistil with three stigmas. After pollination by insects, the pistil ripens, by autumn, to a greyish white, papery capsule bearing three reflexed points or horns. Within this lie several small, hard black seeds, which escape when the capsule splits. When they sprout in the following spring, each seed raises two oval seed-leaves, which wither and fall after one summer's growth;

normal evergreen foliage then follows.

Never a tall tree, box may develop a trunk about 15cm (6in) in diameter, clad in thin, corky bark broken into pale brown squares, like the skin of a crocodile. Box wood is bright orange-yellow, very hard, heavy and stable. Before the advent of plastics, it was widely used for rulers, mathematical instruments, surgical aids and household utensils. It is still a favourite medium for the finest wood sculpture. Many fine illustrations were once printed with boxwood blocks: the boxwood end grain provided fine texture and long wear.

Common hornbeam
Carpinus betulus
The beautiful yellow-green and purple speckled catkins appear with the new leaves.

Common hornbeam
Carpinus betulus
Leaves are doubly serrate with marked veins. Seeds in bunches of pale green bracts.

Hornbeams *(Carpinus)*

A genus of about 20 species, horn-beams grow in the northern temper-ate zone and are at their best in rich soil on low ground. Superficially, they are similar in appearance to birches, but they have readily distinguished charac-teristics. The alternate leaves are sharp-pointed and finely serrated, the catkins are enclosed in buds during the winter; and the small nut-like fruits are enclosed in three-pointed bracts that hang in bunches. The boles, which are elliptical rather than circular, tend to become fluted. The timber is very hard, horny and cross-grained.

Common hornbeam *(Carpinus betulus)*
Native to Europe and Asia Minor, this species grows to about 25m (80ft) tall, with sinuous ascending branches and an irregular crown. The bark is silver-grey striped with fawn, and develops rather large flat ridges; the boles of old trees are deeply fluted, eccentric and twisted. The slender buds are closely appressed and sharp pointed. The leaves are oblong-obovate, pointed, 7–10cm (3–4in) long, sharply double-toothed, with about 15 pairs of conspicuous parallel veins, becoming golden in the autumn. Abun-dant yellow-green catkins, 3–10cm

Common hornbeam
Carpinus betulus
A broad, densely branched
crown with many ascending
branches, shown here in summer
and winter.

(1¼–4in) long, appear in spring. The fruit forms in hanging clusters of green bracts, about 3cm (1¼in) long, enclosing ribbed nutlets (6mm/¼in).

The greyish cream timber, very hard and tough, was once used for such things as ox-yokes, cogs for watermills, and butcher's blocks, or was dyed black as an ebony substitute. Common hornbeam was often grown as coppice for firewood.

There are many cultivars of common hornbeam, including two good street

trees: 'Fastigiata', syn. 'Pyramidalis', of pyramidal form with many ascending branches, and 'Columnaris', of very narrow form.

American hornbeam
(Carpinus caroliniana)
An eastern North American tree, seldom above 13m (43ft) tall, this species has characteristics similar to common hornbeam (*Carpinus betulus*) but is broader in form and has oval buds and very attractive autumn colours.

Bitternut
Carya cordiformis
An irregular, rather narrow,
not very dense crown.
Mid-green foliage, shown
here in summer. Trunk
seldom very stout.

Hickories *(Carya)*

The hickories are closely related to the walnuts but they are more graceful, usually of narrower form, and the crowns are less dense. If a twig of walnut is slit open with a knife, its chambered pith is visible, while in the hickories the pith is solid.

There are about 22 species of hickory, nearly all of which originate in North America, particularly in the large forest areas of the eastern States.

In general, the hickories have alternate buds and compound serrate leaves with 3 to 17 leaflets, the foliage giving rich golden autumn colours. Male flowers are in the form of three-pronged catkins, and female flowers are clustered at the top of new shoots. The nuts are usually smaller than walnuts, often more pointed, and with four grooves or narrow wings on the husks.

Bitternut *(Carya cordiformis)*
This tree is one of the hardiest of all the hickories. It is the most common hickory

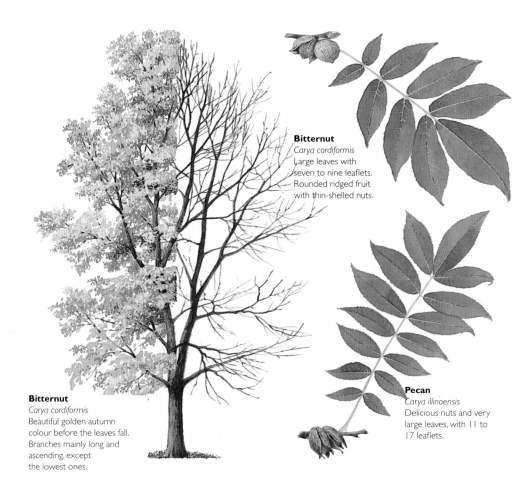

Bitternut
Carya cordiformis
Large leaves with
seven to nine leaflets.
Rounded ridged fruit
with thin-shelled nuts.

Pecan
Carya illinoensis
Delicious nuts and very
large leaves, with 11 to
17 leaflets.

Bitternut
Carya cordiformis
Beautiful golden autumn
colour before the leaves fall.
Branches mainly long and
ascending, except
the lowest ones.

in North America, ranging all over the central and eastern states north to Quebec and northern Wisconsin. Its special feature is its curving yellow winter buds. The leaves have seven to nine sub-sessile leaflets, the middle pair being the longest, turning golden in autumn; the bark is finely ridged.

Pecan *(Carya illinoensis)*
A large and splendid tree but the least hardy of all the hickories, this is a native of the Mississippi basin and is difficult to grow at all in Europe further north than central France. The leaves are very large, up to 80cm (32in) long, with 13 to 17 graceful curving leaflets; the bark is rough and fissured. The oblong nuts are delicious and in great demand.

Big shell bark hickory *(Carya laciniosa)*
The bark of this species flakes away in curiously overlaid curving scales. The leaves of big shell bark hickory are particularly large, up to 80cm (32in); they turn yellow in autumn, and usually have seven leaflets. The nuts are similar to those of shagbark hickory (*Carya ovata*) but not as palatable. The big shell bark hickory is native to the USA, from western New York to Iowa, and from Michigan to Tennessee.

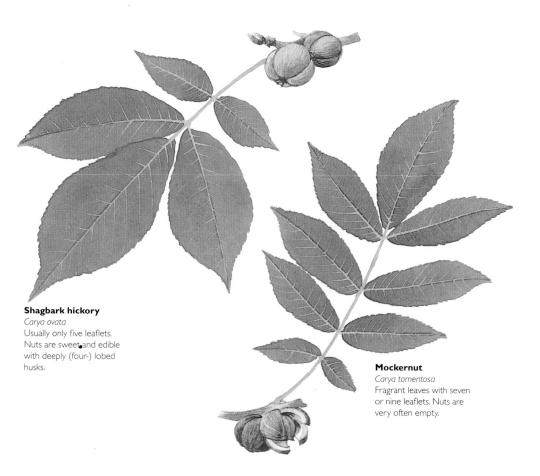

Shagbark hickory
Carya ovata
Usually only five leaflets.
Nuts are sweet and edible
with deeply (four-) lobed
husks.

Mockernut
Carya tomentosa
Fragrant leaves with seven
or nine leaflets. Nuts are
very often empty.

Shagbark hickory (*Carya ovata*)

This tree is native to eastern USA and the mountains of northeast Mexico. As its name implies, it is the bark that makes this species easy to identify; at about 25 years it starts becoming shaggy and flaking. On old trees, the bark is particularly spectacular, with tattered strips curling away in all directions — a feature that may help to prevent squirrels from getting the nuts too easily. The leaves are large, 45–65cm (18–26in); the leaflets, (usually three to five) are rather hard and thick. The nuts are very good to eat and about 4cm (1½in) in diameter.

Mockernut or bigbud hickory (*Carya tomentosa*)

As one of the common names indicates, the buds of this tree are large, 2 x 1.5cm (¾ x ½in) or even larger, and densely hairy. The nuts, approximately 4cm (1½in) in diameter, are very often empty. The large leaves, up to 50cm (20in), are fragrant, with seven leaflets, and turn deep gold in autumn. Its timber is of high quality, and the bark is only slightly fissured. Mockernut or bigbud hickory is widely distributed in southeastern USA, particularly in the Mississippi, Missouri and Ohio basins.

Sweet chestnut
Castanea sativa
A magnificent tree, shown here
in summer and winter, preferring
warmer sites.

Sweet Chestnuts *(Castanea)*

Ten species of this genus grow in the temperate regions, but the devastating chestnut blight bark disease (*Endothea parasitica*) has already virtually wiped out the American *Castanea dentata* and is a serious threat to other sweet chestnuts around the world, particularly Europe. All sweet chestnut species prefer warm sites and grow best on light soils and sunny aspects.

Sweet chestnuts are stately trees that live to five hundred years or sometimes longer. The bark starts smooth and brown, but soon splits into longer spiralling fissures. The nuts, growing in sharp-prickled husks, two or three together, are large and in warm climates provide a popular and nutritious food.

Japanese chestnut (*Castanea crenata*)
A small Japanese tree, fairly resistant to blight, with leaves nearly as large as in the sweet or Spanish chestnut (*Castanea sativa*) but having grey down on the underside. The original stock has poor nuts, but special strains have been developed, giving excellent crops widely used in Japan.

Chinese chestnut
(*Castanea mollissima*)
This species from China and Korea grows

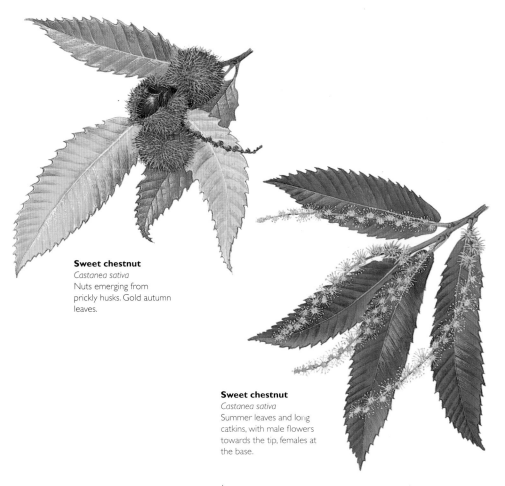

Sweet chestnut
Castanea sativa
Nuts emerging from
prickly husks. Gold autumn
leaves.

Sweet chestnut
Castanea sativa
Summer leaves and long
catkins, with male flowers
towards the tip, females at
the base.

to about 20m (70ft) and is the most
resistant to chestnut blight. Both leaves
and nuts of the Chinese chestnut are
smaller than those of the sweet or Spanish chestnut (*Castanea sativa*).

Sweet or Spanish chestnut
(*Castanea sativa*)

A native of southern Europe, western
Asia and North Africa, this large, handsome tree grows to 35m (120ft) tall with
girths of up to 13m (43ft). It was introduced to Britain by the Romans because
polenta (chestnut meal) was a staple
ration for their soldiers. The bark is
deeply fissured into long ridges, often

spirally arranged. It has large, glossy
green, hard textured leaves, up to 20cm
x 9cm (8 x 3½in), sharply serrate and
with prominent parallel veins. The heavily scented, cord-like, pale yellow
catkins, 16–25cm (6–10in) long, appear
in summer. The glossy brown nuts, held
in tough, prickly green husks, are eaten
raw, or used in cooking in a number of
ways: roasted, boiled or crystallized into
'marrons glacés'.

The light brown timber may be
offered as 'oak' but is not as strong as
oak, and lacks the medullary rays that
give oak its beautiful grain.

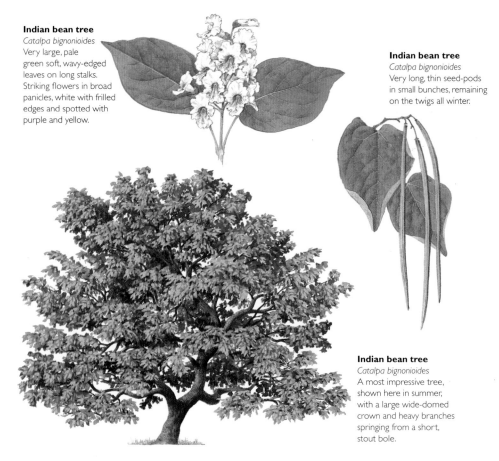

Indian bean tree
Catalpa bignonioides
Very large, pale green soft, wavy-edged leaves on long stalks. Striking flowers in broad panicles, white with frilled edges and spotted with purple and yellow.

Indian bean tree
Catalpa bignonioides
Very long, thin seed-pods in small bunches, remaining on the twigs all winter.

Indian bean tree
Catalpa bignonioides
A most impressive tree, shown here in summer, with a large wide-domed crown and heavy branches springing from a short, stout bole.

Indian Bean Tree *(Catalpa bignonioides)*

The genus *Catalpa* consists of a few very attractive species from North America, eastern Asia and the West Indies. They are noted for their very large leaves and long, slender seed-pods.

Indian bean tree *(Catalpa bignonioides)* A magnificent tree from southeastern USA, reaching 20m (70ft) tall, often wider than it is high, with large spreading branches and a broad domed crown. The twigs are stout, pithy in the centre, with large leaf scars; the light green leaves are bright and very large, up to 25cm x 20cm (10 x 8in), often in whorls of three, entire, rounded with a short point, and soft with a slightly wavy edge. The beautiful flowers are very like those of horse chestnut (*Aesculus*), but are borne in broader panicles, with larger individual bell-shaped flowers with frilled edges and yellow and purple spots. They are produced in masses on older trees in midsummer. The slender, dark brown seed-pods, 14–40cm (5½–16in) long, hang in bunches and tend to stay on the tree all winter. The bark is pinkish brown when young, but on old trees becomes greyer, fissured into small irregular plates. There is a particularly striking golden-leaved cultivar, 'Aurea'.

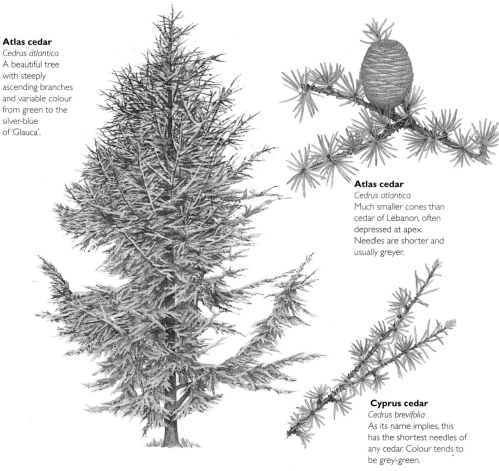

Atlas cedar
Cedrus atlantica
A beautiful tree with steeply ascending branches and variable colour from green to the silver-blue of 'Glauca'.

Atlas cedar
Cedrus atlantica
Much smaller cones than cedar of Lebanon, often depressed at apex. Needles are shorter and usually greyer.

Cyprus cedar
Cedrus brevifolia
As its name implies, this has the shortest needles of any cedar. Colour tends to be grey-green.

Cedars *(Cedrus)*

The name cedar should really only be used for members of the true cedar family, *Cedrus*, but in various parts of the world all sorts of quite different species are known as cedars, such as junipers, cypresses, thujas, torreyas, cryptomerias, *cedrela* or *libocedrus* (now called *calocedrus* or *austrocedrus*). We shall consider here a closely related group of four *Cedrus* species from the Mediterranean and the Himalayas. These share the following features: the needles are arranged in two ways, just like larches (*Larix*), singly on the growing shoots but in tufts of 10 to 20 all together on older twigs (unlike larches, cedars are evergreen). In contrast to most conifers, the true cedars flower in autumn. Their barrel-shaped cones are upright and disintegrate while still on the branches, producing winged seeds and leaving behind the central axis of the cone on the tree.

Atlas or Algerian cedar
(Cedrus atlantica)
From the Atlas Mountains of Algeria and Morocco, this is a tree of narrower, more upright habit, hardier than other true cedars, with fairly short needles, 1–3cm (½–1¼in), usually rather blue-green and

Deodar cedar
Cedrus deodara
Barrel-shaped cones like cedar of Lebanon, but they feel lumpy and are often larger. Needles are longer than on other cedars.

Deodar cedar
Cedrus deodara
A very fine evergreen tree with level or drooping branches and pendulous end shoots.

in the case of 'Glauca', very widely used in parks and gardens, a wonderful silver-blue colour. The growing twigs tend to ascend. The male flowers, about 4cm (1½in) high, are pinkish yellow when ripe; the female flowers are less purple than those of Lebanon cedar (*Cedrus libani*). The cones are smaller, 5–8cm (2–3in) long. Atlas cedars grow better on alkaline soils than the other true cedars.

Cyprus cedar
(*Cedrus brevifolia*)
This tree from Cyprus, seldom more than 18m (60ft) high, has level branches and green or blue-green very short needles,

about 1cm (½in) long. The cones, measuring up to 10cm x 5cm (4 x 2in), are more tapered.

Deodar cedar (*Cedrus deodara*)
This is a tall tree, exceeding 60m (200ft) in height on the best sites, with a girth up to 12m (40ft). It is found growing at high altitudes in the western Himalayas and Afghanistan. The Deodar is narrower and more conical than the Lebanon (*Cedrus libani*). The growing shoots droop gracefully and a young tree is indeed a most beautiful sight. The green to silvery green needles are long, 3–6cm (1¼–2½in), and narrow. The cones are

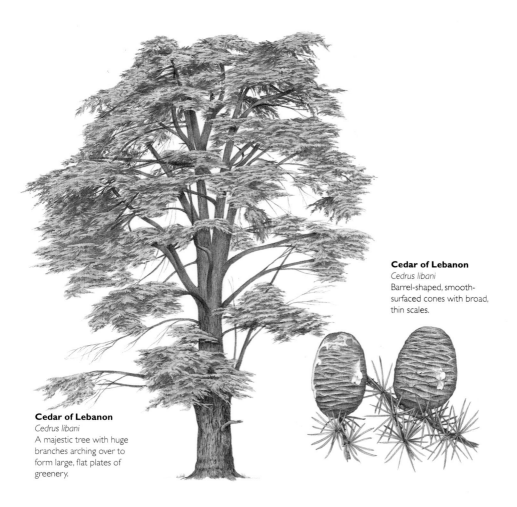

Cedar of Lebanon
Cedrus libani
Barrel-shaped, smooth-
surfaced cones with broad,
thin scales.

Cedar of Lebanon
Cedrus libani
A majestic tree with huge
branches arching over to
form large, flat plates of
greenery.

less abundant than on the other true cedars and larger, up to 14cm (5½in) tall, with broad scales that are more ridged than the others.

Cedar of Lebanon *(Cedrus libani)*

There are only a few cedar of Lebanon groves left, mainly at high altitudes, but they contain some immense trees up to 14m (46ft) in diameter. Their age tends to be exaggerated, often quoted as being over 2,500 years, but this species is a fast grower, and trees of only 150 years already assume an air of timeless dignity, reaching up to 40m (130ft) high with huge boles and magnificent flat-topped crowns over the massive lower branches. They tend to break up with age and few reach even 1,000 years. The needles, 2–3cm (¾–1¼in) long, vary from dark green to a fairly blue-green. The male flowers are erect, 3–5cm (1¼–2in) tall, and grey-green before they shed their yellow pollen, while the females, also erect but only 1cm (½in) long, are green at first, purple when ripe. The barrel-shaped cones are up to 14cm x 7cm (5½ x 3in), the broad flat scales having purple edges and often being resinous, and the seeds have broad wings. The dark grey bark fissures into short scaly ridges.

Judas tree
Cercis siliquastrum
The beautiful rosy-pink, pea-type flowers occur in clusters on the branches.

Eastern American redbud
Cercis canadensis
Larger and more pointed leaves than the Judas tree.

Judas tree
Cercis siliquastrum
Typical round leaves, deeply notched at the base. Seed-pods at the beautiful purple stage.

Redbuds and Judas Tree *(Cercis)*

Cercis is a small genus of seven species from North America, southern Europe and East Asia. Trees in this genus have alternate, simple leaves that are rounded, heart-shaped at the base, and with five or seven prominent veins. An unusual feature is that the pink, pea-type flowers occur in clusters on quite thick branches, or on the trunk itself, as well as on younger shoots.

Eastern American redbud
(Cercis canadensis)
Very similar to Judas tree (*Cercis siliquastrum*), but the leaves are larger and more pointed, the flowers slightly smaller, and the tree of narrower form. It is one of the most beautiful American trees and common in the eastern and central states. 'Alba' is a white cultivar.

Chinese redbud *(Cercis chinensis)*
The largest of all the redbuds, sometimes reaching 20m (70ft), the Chinese redbud is very similar to the eastern American redbud (*Cercis canadensis*), but its leaves are less glaucous beneath, the flowers a little larger, and the seed-pods bigger and more pointed. It is a more tender species than most of the others.

Western redbud *(Cercis occidentalis)*
The western redbud is native to Califor-

Judas tree
Cercis siliquastrum
Round-headed, dense
crown of the Judas tree,
shown here in late
summer. The purple seed-
pods show up against
the dark green foliage.

nia, with both leaves and flowers very
like those of the Judas tree (*Cercis siliquastrum*). It is smaller than the eastern
American redbud (*C. canadensis*).

Cercis racemosa

This Chinese tree grows up to 10m (30ft)
tall, with lovely rose-pink flowers hanging in racemes up to 10cm (4in) long,
each consisting of 20 to 40 blossoms. Its
young twigs are distinct in that they are
very downy.

Judas tree *(Cercis siliquastrum)*

Native to southern Europe and western
Asia, the Judas tree is the species most
often seen in European parks and gar-

dens, growing to about 12m (40ft) but
usually of rather bushy habit with
rounded crown and, on older trees,
drooping branches. The buds are dark
red, the leaves round, 6–10cm (2½–4in)
across, dark green above, glaucous
beneath, and with green and red stalks.
Bright rosy-pink flowers in small
bunches cover the tree in spring – a wonderful sight. The flat seed-pods, about 8 x
2cm (3 x ¾in), usually in large numbers,
are beautifully coloured, passing from
green to purple and finally light brown;
they are a special feature of the species.
'Alba' is a pretty white-flowered cultivar.

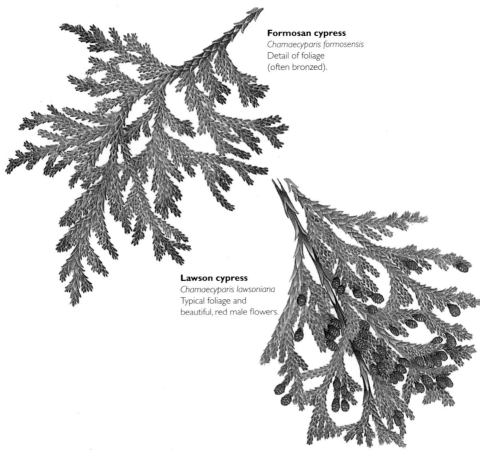

Formosan cypress
Chamaecyparis formosensis
Detail of foliage
(often bronzed).

Lawson cypress
Chamaecyparis lawsoniana
Typical foliage and
beautiful, red male flowers.

Neo-cypresses *(Chamaecyparis)*

This is a group of six species, whose foliage is flattened so that each twiglet is broader than it is thick. In the 'true' cypresses *(see pp.64–65)* the foliage is rounded or angular.

Formosan cypress

(Chamaecyparis formosensis)

This is a huge tree, which in its native forests reaches a height of 53m (170ft) with a diameter up to 2m (6ft), but in other countries it seldom grows to any great size and is usually only planted as an ornamental. Its foliage is dull green tinged with bronze, and curved downwards at the tips of the shoots.

Lawson cypress or Port Orford cedar

(Chamaecyparis lawsoniana)

This is well scattered through the forests of southwest Oregon and northwest California, but it is increasingly being planted in other countries. It will grow in almost any soil, is very hardy, transplants well, stands frequent clipping, is easy to propagate and is unusually free from pests and diseases.

It is a large tree, reaching a height of 60m (200ft) in its native forests, with a diameter up to 3m (10ft), and brownish bark fissured into irregular vertical plates. The short, scale-like leaves are

Lawson cypress
Chamaecyparis lawsoniana
'Fletcheri'
Narrow when young but
has multiple leaders later.

Lawson cypress
Chamaecyparis lawsoniana
'Fletcheri'
Has juvenile-type feathery
foliage.

dark green above and paler beneath, somewhat compressed, and strongly scented when crushed. Crimson male flowers, 2–3mm (1/16–1/8in) long, are abundant on the ends of small twigs; female flowers, 5mm (1/4in) long, are slate-blue, turning green. The globular cones are up to 8mm (3/8in) in diameter and woody, with wrinkled scales that turn from a glaucous green finally to brown.

Chamaecyparis lawsoniana is a very variable species, and has given rise to a great number of cultivars covering a wide range of size, shape and colour:
'Fletcheri' has blue-grey feathery juvenile foliage, often with several leaders.
'Columnaris' has a narrow form and dense blue-grey foliage.
'Ellwoodii' is slow growing and slightly wider than 'Columnaris', with steely blue-grey foliage.
'Lutea' is columnar, conical at the top, with golden foliage and is fast growing.
'Pottenii' has a narrow form, tapering at both top and bottom, with dense green foliage and vertical shoots.
'Stewartii' is a golden variety with green older foliage and small arching branches.
'Wisselii' has little turrets of dark bluish green foliage located at the ends of the

Nootka cypress
Chamaecyparis nootkatensis
Conic form with markedly drooping foliage.

Nootka cypress
Chamaecyparis nootkatensis
Typical foliage and cones in the green stage.

branches. It is a narrow-form tree.

Nootka cypress or Alaska cedar
(*Chamaecyparis nootkatensis*)

Native to a narrow coastal belt from Alaska to north Oregon, this large forest tree may grow to 53m (170ft) tall, with a diameter extending to 2m (6ft). It will succeed on poor soils and exposed sites. The foliage is dull green without white markings, and feels rough if rubbed the wrong way; it has a strong smell if crushed. The flat twigs are pendulous. The cones, blue-bloomed at first, brown later, are about 1cm (½in) in diameter, with scales carrying curved-tipped short spines. The bark is fissured into long peeling strips. 'Pendula' has yellowish green foliage and long, pendulous shoots.

Hinoki cypress (*Chamaecyparis obtusa*)
This is a Japanese species growing to 35m (120ft). The branchlets are flattened, with the tips drooping or turned back. The leaves are closely pressed, blunt tipped, with the lateral pairs longer than the others. They are shining green above, patterned with white lines below, and have a sweet resinous scent when crushed. The cones are about 1cm (½in) across, green turning to orange-brown, with a small ridge in the centre of each

Hinoki cypress
Chamaecyparis obtusa
Foliage and ripe cones just opening to release seeds.

Sawara cypress
Chamaecyparis pisifera 'Filifera Aurea'
Conic form and striking golden foliage.

Sawara cypress
Chamaecyparis pisifera
Normal foliage of the green type.

scale. The red-brown bark tends to peel away in soft, stringy, long, shaggy strips. 'Crippsii' has golden foliage and, after initial slow growth, reaches 15m (50ft).

Sawara cypress
(Chamaecyparis pisifera)

This is another Japanese species growing to about the same size as Hinoki cypress (*Chamaecyparis obtusa*). The crown is conic, but often broadened by multiple leaders, while the lower heavy branches sometimes layer at the base. The leaves are a bright shiny green above, marked with white patches below, and the small, closely pressed leaf scales have fine incurved points. The male flowers are very small and pale brown; the female flowers are round, green and about 5mm (¼in) in diameter. The round cones, about 7mm (¼in) in diameter, are grey-green ripening to brown, with small spines on the centre of each scale. The bark is reddish brown, deeply fissured and peels off in long, thin strips.

'Filifera' is a broad, often many-stemmed tree with spreading branches and thin, cord-like pendulous twigs with small bunches of scattered dark green side-shoots. 'Filifera Aurea' has golden young shoots.

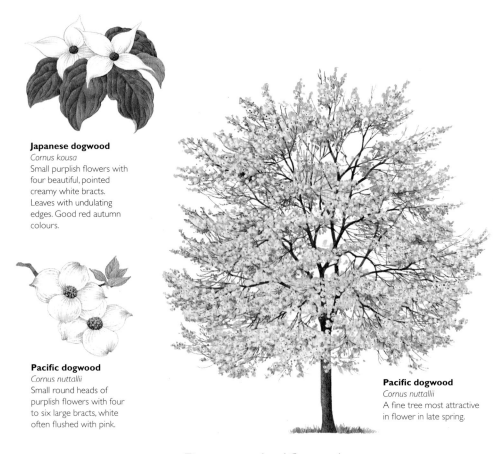

Japanese dogwood
Cornus kousa
Small purplish flowers with
four beautiful, pointed
creamy white bracts.
Leaves with undulating
edges. Good red autumn
colours.

Pacific dogwood
Cornus nuttallii
Small round heads of
purplish flowers with four
to six large bracts, white
often flushed with pink.

Pacific dogwood
Cornus nuttallii
A fine tree most attractive
in flower in late spring.

Dogwoods *(Cornus)*

This outstandingly beautiful group, comprising about 40 species in all, is particularly well represented in America, but also grows in Europe, Siberia, China, Japan and the Himalayas. Most dogwoods have opposite leaves with veins arching towards the leaf-tip, small four-parted flowers, often backed by large showy pink or white bracts, ornamental berries and sometimes beautiful coloured stems.

Cornus alba

This is a fine red-stemmed dogwood from Siberia, with bluish white berries. There is a particularly good type, 'Westonbirt Dogwood', with extra brilliant red stems.

Asiatic dogwood *(Cornus controversa)*
This beautiful species comes from China, the Himalayas and Japan. It forms a large tree, up to 20m (70ft), with remarkable, slender, horizontal branches and, unlike most dogwoods, alternate leaves; it has masses of white flowers.

Flowering dogwood *(Cornus florida)*
Native to eastern USA, this is a slightly smaller tree that grows up to 15m (50ft), giving a mass of white- or pink-bracted flowers and good autumn colours.

Japanese dogwood *(Cornus kousa)*
This is a free-flowering shrub or small tree, up to 8m (25ft) tall, with beautiful,

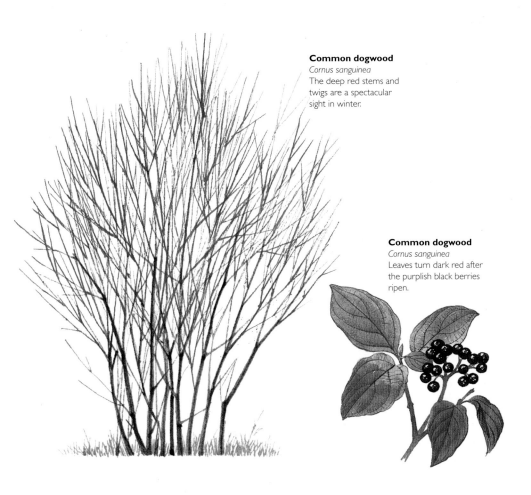

Common dogwood
Cornus sanguinea
The deep red stems and
twigs are a spectacular
sight in winter.

Common dogwood
Cornus sanguinea
Leaves turn dark red after
the purplish black berries
ripen.

slightly twisted, creamy white or pinkish pointed bracts, four per flower, and excellent autumn colours. Its special features are its strange fruits, yellow at first then turning red like round hard raspberries on stalks up to 7cm (3in) long.

Cornelian cherry *(Cornus mas)*

This striking European species is often bushy but sometimes up to 8m (25ft) high, and loved for its little bunches of small yellow flowers in late winter to early spring on the leafless stems, and its bright red berries up to 2cm (¾in) long.

Pacific dogwood *(Cornus nuttallii)*

The biggest of the American dogwoods, this species forms a magnificent tree, up to 30m (100ft) tall, with large white bracts to its flowers and wonderful gold and scarlet colours in autumn.

Common dogwood or cornel
(Cornus sanguinea)

This dogwood, the main native species in Europe, is remarkable for its striking red stems, beautiful autumn colours and glossy black berries. It does well on alkaline soils and there is a variegated form commonly used in gardens.

Cornus stolonifera

From North America this is red-stemmed, with dark purplish red twigs.

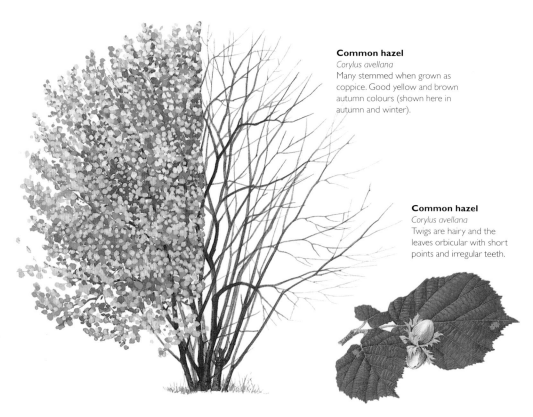

Common hazel
Corylus avellana
Many stemmed when grown as
coppice. Good yellow and brown
autumn colours (shown here in
autumn and winter).

Common hazel
Corylus avellana
Twigs are hairy and the
leaves orbicular with short
points and irregular teeth.

Hazels *(Corylus)*

All 15 species of this genus of deciduous trees and shrubs occur in the northern temperate regions. They have alternate, toothed leaves, male and female flowers on the same tree, with all male flowers in pendent catkins.

American hazel *(Corylus americana)*
This shrub, up to 4m (12ft), from eastern North America, is very like common European hazel *(Corylus avellana)*, but has poorer, slightly flattened nuts enclosed in very long involucres.

Common hazel or cobnut
(Corylus avellana)
Native to Europe, Western Asia and North Africa, this small tree has small brown ovoid buds set on distinctly hairy twigs, opening to give irregularly toothed, rounded leaves 5–9cm (2–3½in) long, downy on both surfaces. In their short, unopened form, the male catkins can be seen all winter, growing up to 7cm (3in) long, pale yellow with golden pollen blowing in the wind. The female flowers are plump little upright greenish buds, 3–5mm (⅛–¼in) long, tipped with vivid crimson styles; the nuts, one to four together, each in a leafy cup, are pale green at first, ripening to golden brown.

The cultivar 'Contorta', known as

Beaked hazel
Corylus cornuta
Leaves are slightly smaller than in filbert, but bracts extend in a long point beyond the nut.

Purple-leafed filbert
Corylus maxima 'Purpurea'
Has very dark purple leaves and contrasts well with other shrubs.

Filbert
Corylus maxima
Larger in both leaf and nut than common hazel. The nuts are enclosed by bracts.

corkscrew hazel, is an ornamental, slow-growing shrub with strangely twisted twigs and branches.

Chinese hazel (*Corylus chinensis*)

Another large tree, this is similar to Turkish hazel (*Corylus colurna*) but native to central and western China.

Turkish hazel (*Corylus colurna*)

A fine tree, native to southeastern Europe and Asia Minor, the largest of the group and of stately pyramidal form. Turkish hazel grows up to 25m (80ft) tall. It has brown scaly bark, large leaves up to 14cm (5½in) long, and clusters of edible nuts covered by whiskery husks.

Beaked hazel

(*Corylus cornuta* syn. *C. rostrata*)

This shrub from eastern and central USA seldom grows above 3m (10ft) high, with long, bristly, beaked husks protruding 2–4cm (¾–1½in) beyond the nuts.

Filbert (*Corylus maxima*)

Native to southern Europe, this tree closely resembles the common hazel (*Corylus avellana*), except that it grows taller and has larger, superior nuts enclosed in very long husks. There are various strains planted for nut crops in southern Europe and in California, and a purple-leaved cultivar, 'Purpurea'.

Purple Venetian sumac
Cotinus coggygria
'Atropurpureus'
Simil0, young shoots and
inflorescences are all purple.

Venetian sumac
Cotinus coggygria
Shown here in summer,
Venetian sumac is covered
in hairy, feathery panicles
that look like smoke as
they move in the wind.

Venetian Sumac *(Cotinus coggygria)*

This genus of some 150 species belongs to the great cashew family, Anacardiaceae. Its leaves may be large and pinnate or simple; some are deciduous, some are evergreen and several are rather poisonous.

Venetian sumac, smoke tree or wig tree
(Cotinus coggygria syn. *Rhus cotinus)*
This species is often called 'smoke tree' or 'wig tree' because of its remarkable hairy, feathery inflorescent panicles, which are pink at first then turn grey, giving a 'smoky' appearance to the whole

bush. Native to central and southern Europe, it usually forms a rounded bush up to 4m (12ft) high, with simple obovate or orbicular leaves, about 4–8cm (1½–3in) long, with well-marked parallel veins and thin stalks. The loose panicles bear no flowers and are simply a mass of silky hairs; the leaves turn yellow in late autumn. A strong yellow dye is obtained from the twigs.

There is a cultivar 'Atropurpureus', known as Purple Venetian sumac, with purple leaves, twigs and panicles.

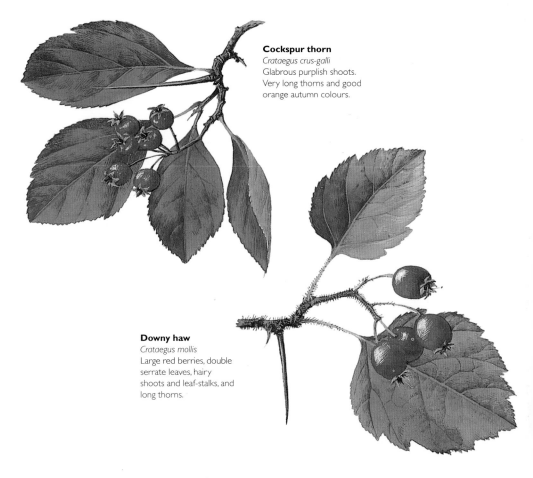

Cockspur thorn
Crataegus crus-galli
Glabrous purplish shoots.
Very long thorns and good
orange autumn colours.

Downy haw
Crataegus mollis
Large red berries, double
serrate leaves, hairy
shoots and leaf-stalks, and
long thorns.

Hawthorns *(Crataegus)*

The hawthorns are a small section within the very large *Crataegus* or thorns group, which contains several hundred species, mostly American, many of them only shrubs and outside the range of this book. The hawthorns included here will introduce some of those that become trees.

Cockspur thorn *(Crataegus crus-galli)*
A North American species much used in many countries for street and garden planting, with attractive red berries and unusual rich orange autumn colours. A flat-topped, wide-spreading small tree, seldom more than 6m (20ft) high, with glabrous, obovate, serrate leaves, about 6 x 3cm (2½ x 1¼in), purple-brown twigs with frequent thorns, and white flowers, 1.5cm (½in) in diameter, in erect bunches. There are hybrids between this thorn and others. Some have larger flowers or leaves, others display redder autumn shades.

Crataegus macracanthia
A small eastern North American tree with abundant huge thorns up to 13cm

Crataegus macracanthia
A sketch of the winter twig showing the long thorns, up to 13cm (5in) in length.

Hawthorn
Crataegus monogyna
White flowers with pink anthers. Stipules at base of leaf stalks.

Hawthorn
Crataegus monogyna
A densely branched bush or small tree shown here in late spring, covered in scented snowy flowers, and winter.

(5in) long. It has white flowers, 2cm (¾in) across, with yellow anthers and bright crimson berries about 1cm (½in) in diameter.

Downy or red haw *(Crataegus mollis)*
A small tree from central USA, this has white hairs on young twigs, large, downy leaves, truncate or heart-shaped at the base, 5–12cm (2–5in) long, with glandular-toothed edges; white flowers, 2.5cm (1in) across, on white-hairy stalks; and red, downy berries up to 2.5cm (1in).

Hawthorn, may or quickthorn
(Crataegus monogyna)
Native from Europe right across to Afghanistan, this is the most common of all hedging species, its thorny nature, dense branch growth and ability to withstand constant cutting back making it ideal for that purpose. But left alone it will develop into a small rugged tree up to 15m (50ft) high, with a very strong trunk, often fluted, with bark flaking off in irregular scales. In late spring, hawthorn is covered in snowy white blossom, and the countryside seems filled with its strongly scented whiteness. When mature, the dark shining green leaves are up to about 7 x 5cm (3 x 2in), coarsely toothed, and irregularly lobed,

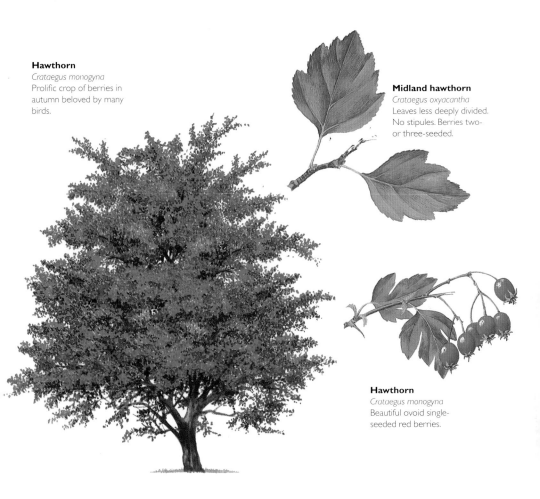

Hawthorn
Crataegus monogyna
Prolific crop of berries in autumn beloved by many birds.

Midland hawthorn
Crataegus oxyacantha
Leaves less deeply divided. No stipules. Berries two- or three-seeded.

Hawthorn
Crataegus monogyna
Beautiful ovoid single-seeded red berries.

with two leafy bracts at the base of the short stalks. The twigs are reddish brown, with straight sharp thorns; the tiny brown buds open into white flowers, 1.5cm (½in) across, in dense bunches; the red berries are abundant, ovoid, about 1cm (½in) long, and single seeded.

Midland hawthorn
(*Crataegus oxyacantha*)
Found mainly in heavy soils and shade in south of England and Europe, this is similar to the hawthorn (*Crataegus monogyna*) but has shallower lobed leaves without bracts at the base of the stalks, and the berries are two- or three-seeded.

Crataegus pinnatifida
China has given us several thorns, this being the best-known. It has long, irregularly lobed leaves with red and gold autumn colours and large red berries, 1.5cm (½in) in diameter, with small dots on the skin. It has a variety, *major*, cultivated for its large red edible berries.

Glastonbury thorn
(*Crataegus praecox* syn. *C. biflora*)
This variety of hawthorn produces some flowers in winter as well as in late spring: this has led to a whole crop of legends, and mythological tales, relating to Glastonbury, southwest England.

Japanese red cedar
Cryptomeria japonica
Twigs carry fairly long,
hard-pointed green scales,
curved inwards. Many
small round cones, rough
with curved spines.

Japanese red cedar
Cryptomeria japonica
A tall, narrowly conic tree,
becomes round topped
when old. Lower branches
sweep down, often layering
on the ground.

Japanese Red Cedar *(Cryptomeria japonica)*

Native to China and Japan, *Cryptomeria japonica* is an unusual tree and the only species in the genus.

Japanese red cedar

(Cryptomeria japonica)

The Japanese red cedar is narrowly conic, with a slightly rounded apex, but gets more parallel-sided with age and grows to a maximum height of about 54m (175ft). With red-brown heartwood and pale yellow sapwood, it is one of the great timber trees, yielding a strong, durable, fragrant, first-class wood used for buildings, joinery, and furniture; many temples are also built with it. The Japanese call it 'sugi', and it is also known as 'peacock pine'. It is fast growing, and the thick, soft, fibrous, reddish brown bark peels away in long strips and is used locally as a roofing material. In Japan it is a favourite avenue tree and is much used in temple grounds and large gardens; in other countries its ornamental value is becoming better known.

The foliage of *Cryptomeria japonica* is fairly similar to that of the giant

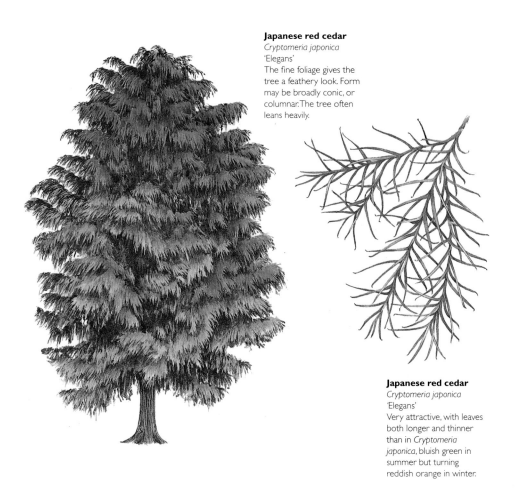

Japanese red cedar
Cryptomeria japonica
'Elegans'
The fine foliage gives the tree a feathery look. Form may be broadly conic, or columnar. The tree often leans heavily.

Japanese red cedar
Cryptomeria japonica
'Elegans'
Very attractive, with leaves both longer and thinner than in *Cryptomeria japonica*, bluish green in summer but turning reddish orange in winter.

sequoia (*Sequoiadendron giganteum*), but the scale-like leaves are longer, more pointed and bend out from the stem more widely in the Japanese red cedar. The colour is a yellower green, the twigs are longer, sparser and more pendulous, and the branches fewer. Yellow male flowers, 3mm (⅛in) in diameter, grow in clusters; the females form small green rosettes. The globular cones are about 2cm (¾in) in diameter, on short stalks, green turning to bright brown.

There is a very popular garden culti-var, 'Elegans', noted for the fact that its long, soft, juvenile-type foliage turns bronze or purple in winter. It has a lax, spreading habit and the lower branches sometimes layer, forming a ring of new trees. There is a smaller, more stable, slower-growing cultivar, 'Elegans Compacta', that is particularly suitable for smaller gardens.

Another cultivar, 'Lobbii', is of nar-rower form, with stiffer branches and an uneven crown, with the twigs tending to be in tufts.

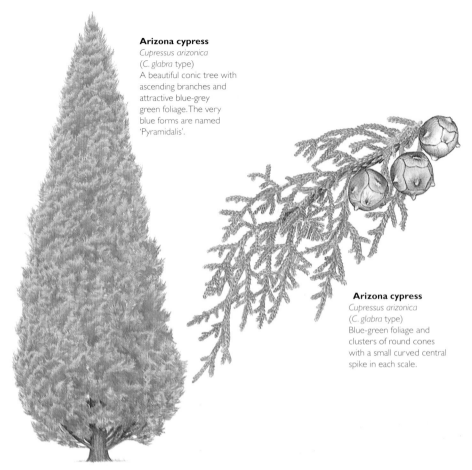

Arizona cypress
Cupressus arizonica
(*C. glabra* type)
A beautiful conic tree with
ascending branches and
attractive blue-grey
green foliage. The very
blue forms are named
'Pyramidalis'.

Arizona cypress
Cupressus arizonica
(*C. glabra* type)
Blue-green foliage and
clusters of round cones
with a small curved central
spike in each scale.

True Cypresses (*Cupressus*)

This is a group of about 20 widely distributed species, in which the foliage is arranged evenly round the twigs to give a rounded or angular section, rather than flattened as in the neo-cypresses (*see* pp.50–53).

Arizona cypress (*Cupressus arizonica*)
A very variable species, both in form and colour, the original type was a medium-sized tree up to 22m (72ft) tall, ovoid-conic in shape. The foliage is grey-green, and the finely fissured bark peels off in thin stringy plates. Botanists have now called the old cultivar 'Bonita' a separate species, *Cupressus glabra*, which has blue-grey foliage and bark flaking off in roundish patches. 'Pyramidalis' is the best ornamental type, with bright silver-blue upswept foliage with a white spot on every leaf and narrow conic form. The clustered cones of all this group are 1.5–2.5cm (½–1in) in diameter.

Mexican cypress or cedar of Goa (*Cupressus lusitanica*)
This is not a cedar and was never a native of Goa, but comes from Mexico and Guatemala, where it grows to a height of 30m (100ft). It has rather pendulous twigs and a fairly wide conic form, usually with a single stem, whose

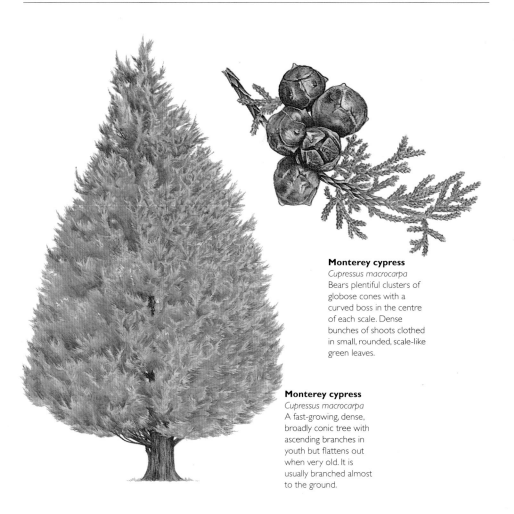

Monterey cypress
Cupressus macrocarpa
Bears plentiful clusters of globose cones with a curved boss in the centre of each scale. Dense bunches of shoots clothed in small, rounded, scale-like green leaves.

Monterey cypress
Cupressus macrocarpa
A fast-growing, dense, broadly conic tree with ascending branches in youth but flattens out when very old. It is usually branched almost to the ground.

branches are more open than Monterey cypress (*Cupressus macrocarpa*). Its special feature is the conspicuously glaucous young cones about 1.5cm (½in) in diameter. The foliage is dark greyish green, the scale-like leaves having spreading acute tips.

Monterey cypress
(Cupressus macrocarpa)

Originating from very small sea-cliff areas at Point Lobos and Cypress Point near Monterey, California, this large, quickly growing cypress has been widely planted as an ornamental, shelter-belt or hedge tree in very many countries. How-

ever, it is subject to damage by severe winters or hard spring frosts, and is rather unreliable when planted away from the sea. It will reach 30m (100ft) in 40 years but seldom exceeds about 37m (125ft). On windswept coasts it becomes gaunt and ragged but under more sheltered conditions it is a fairly broad conic, or rather narrow columnar tree that finally flattens out at the top almost like a Lebanon cedar (*Cedrus libani*). The short, scale-like leaves are closely pressed to the twigs in four rows, darkish green and lemon-scented when crushed. The nearly round cones are 2.5–4cm

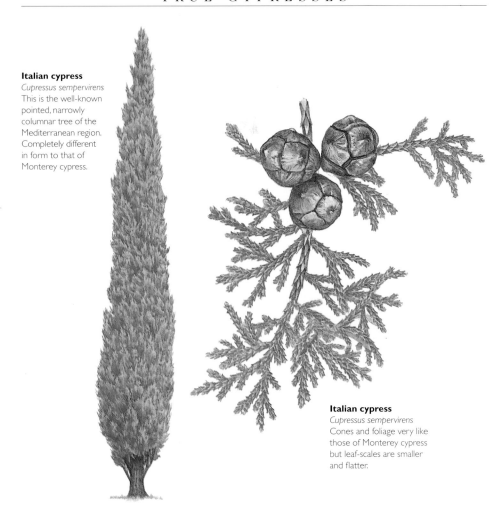

Italian cypress
Cupressus sempervirens
This is the well-known
pointed, narrowly
columnar tree of the
Mediterranean region.
Completely different
in form to that of
Monterey cypress.

Italian cypress
Cupressus sempervirens
Cones and foliage very like
those of Monterey cypress
but leaf-scales are smaller
and flatter.

(1–1½in) long, with large scales with curved bosses in the centre of each one. The seeds have small warts on the surface. The trunk is large and often divided halfway up; the bark is grey-brown and shallowly fissured into an irregular network of plates.

'Lutea' has dullish gold foliage. It is a fast grower, and is very resistant to salt winds. Two brighter gold ornamental trees are 'Goldcrest' and 'Donard Gold'.

Italian cypress
(*Cupressus sempervirens*)

This tree, the classic cypress of Mediter-ranean scenery, is without doubt the best known of all the cypresses, with its slim, dark green, pointed columns rising spire-like to as much as 50m (160ft) among associated trees and shrubs. It is too tender to withstand more northern climates and only succeeds in the milder parts of Britain.

The Italian cypress is similar to the Monterey cypress (*Cupressus macrocarpa*), differing only in its narrower form, smaller, more closely pressed leaves, less strong scent, and seeds with relatively few or no warts on them.

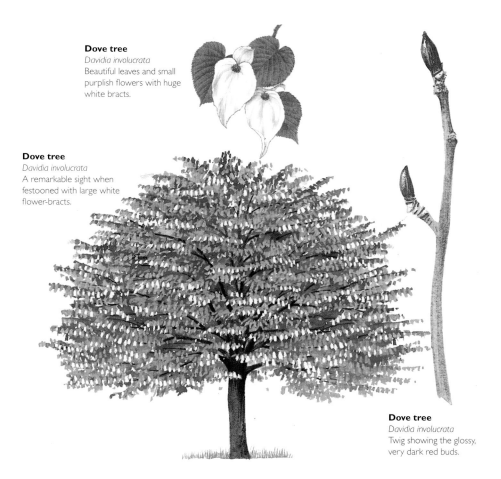

Dove tree
Davidia involucrata
Beautiful leaves and small purplish flowers with huge white bracts.

Dove tree
Davidia involucrata
A remarkable sight when festooned with large white flower-bracts.

Dove tree
Davidia involucrata
Twig showing the glossy, very dark red buds.

Dove Tree *(Davidia involucrata)*

There is a single species in the genus *Davidia*, commonly known as the dove tree. Dove trees are from central and western China, and are closely related to tupelos (*Nyssa sinensis* and *N. sylvatica*).

Dove tree, ghost tree, handkerchief tree (*Davidia involucrata*)

The dove tree grows to a maximum of about 20m (70ft), conical at first but later with a high domed crown and radiating branches, the upper ones ascending, the lower ones level. Its unique feature is the enormous white bracts, which dwarf the small, sweetly scented flowers with purple stamens, and may be as large as 22 x 11cm (9 x 4½in). The cordate, veined leaves are broadly ovate with pointed ends, up to 16 x 13cm (6 x 5in), coarsely toothed and with white pubescence on the underside, often growing in small clusters. The dove tree has unusual shiny, deep red ovoid buds, about 1.5cm (½in) long. The ribbed fruits, about 3 x 2.5cm (1¼ x 1in), are on long stalks and are green at first, later turning purple. The bark is grey-brown, and tends to flake off in small pieces.

The variety *vilmoriniana* differs in having glabrous leaves.

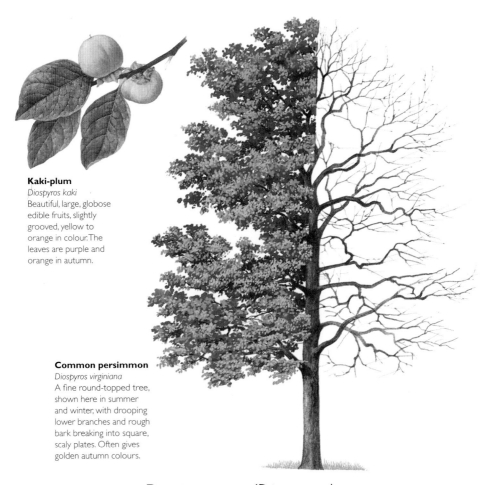

Kaki-plum
Diospyros kaki
Beautiful, large, globose edible fruits, slightly grooved, yellow to orange in colour. The leaves are purple and orange in autumn.

Common persimmon
Diospyros virginiana
A fine round-topped tree, shown here in summer and winter, with drooping lower branches and rough bark breaking into square, scaly plates. Often gives golden autumn colours.

Persimmons *(Diospyros)*

Persimmons form a large group of mostly tropical and evergreen trees, although some of them are deciduous; all persimmons are members of the Ebony family (Ebenaceae).

Kaki-plum or Chinese persimmon
(Diospyros kaki)

Growing to 15m (50ft) tall, this Chinese tree has the best fruits of any of the temperate region persimmons — up to 7cm (3in) in diameter, orange coloured, and much better tasting than the others. Kaki-plum is grown for its fruit, but its timber is inferior to that of common persimmon (*Diospyros virginiana*). The leaves are much larger, 12–24cm (4–10in) long, and pubescent beneath.

Date-plum *(Diospyros lotus)*

This is a broad, dome-shaped evergreen tree, up to 14m (46ft) high, from China and Japan and across to western Asia. It has luxuriant, glossy, dark green, oblong-ovate leaves, on short stalks, varying in size according to the age of the tree; on young trees they may be up to 18 x 5cm (7 x 2in), but they are much smaller and

Common persimmon
Diospyros virginiana
Thick, glossy, pointed oval leaves. Small, four-lobed yellowish flowers on very short stalks.

Common persimmon
Diospyros virginiana
Medium-sized, round edible fruits, yellow to orange with a red cheek.

broader on older specimens. The bark is dull grey and fissured into rectangular squarish plates. Male and female flowers are on separate trees, both types are urn-shaped, cream and pink, and only about 7mm (¼in) long, the males two or three together, the females singly but closely placed in lines. The round fruits, 1–2cm (½–¾in) in diameter, are yellow and purple, and are unpalatable.

Common persimmon
(Diospyros virginiana)
This American species reaches up to 22m (76ft) tall, with the lower branches often rather pendulous and the leaves similar to those of the date-plum (*Diospyros lotus*), though more pubescent beneath and with slightly tougher stalks. The flowers are longer, up to 1.5cm (½in), and the fruits much larger, 2–4cm (¾–1½in) in diameter, pale orange, often with a red cheek, and edible though of rather poor flavour. Old trees have attractive dark grey bark fissured into rectangular blocks. The timber is like ebony.

Common beech
Fagus sylvatica
A truly magnificent tree, shown here in summer, with a dense rounded crown and wide-spreading branches.

American beech
Fagus grandifolia
Toothed leaves, wedge-shaped at the base.

Beeches *(Fagus)*

There are only ten species in this genus, all growing in northern temperate regions, but they include some very important trees. All are deciduous, the leaves, developing from long, slender buds are alternate and parallel-veined, and in most species turn an attractive bronze colour in autumn. Male flowers open in bunches on slender stalks, and the nuts form in four-lobed woody husks. The bark is smooth and the dense, even-grained timber is very valuable.

Siebold's beech
(Fagus crenata syn. sieboldii)
Another Japanese species larger than Japanese beech (*Fagus japonica*), this has a longer, straighter trunk. It is closely allied to common beech (*Fagus sylvatica*) but is distinguished by long strap-like bristles at the base of the nut husks.

Chinese beech *(Fagus englerana)*
This beautiful tree, seldom above 20m (70ft) tall, is from central China. It has very slender long buds, sea-green leaves with deckled wavy edges, turning to fine orange, brown and gold in autumn.

American beech
(Fagus grandifolia syn. F. ferruginea)
The only beech native to America, where it is found mainly in the eastern area,

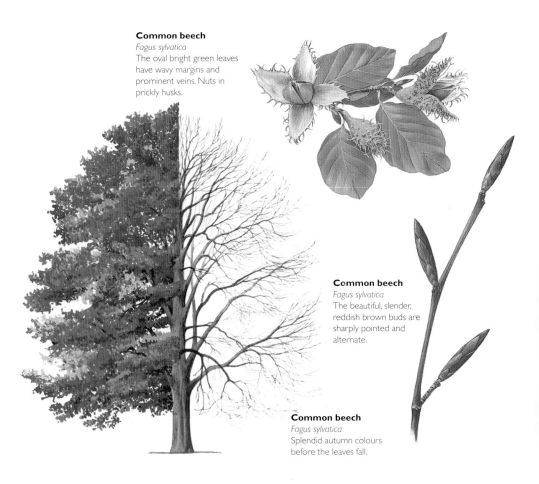

Common beech
Fagus sylvatica
The oval bright green leaves
have wavy margins and
prominent veins. Nuts in
prickly husks.

Common beech
Fagus sylvatica
The beautiful, slender,
reddish brown buds are
sharply pointed and
alternate.

Common beech
Fagus sylvatica
Splendid autumn colours
before the leaves fall.

this is a fine tree, almost as large as common beech (*Fagus sylvatica*), with larger, more pointed leaves up to 13cm (5in) long with coarsely serrate edges and silver-grey bark, often blotched with dark patches. Sucker growth is common in this species.

Japanese beech
(*Fagus japonica*)

The Japanese beech can grow up to 25m (80ft) tall, but with a short bole quickly dividing into several sizeable branches. The beech nuts protrude beyond their husks for approximately two-thirds of their length.

Oriental beech (*Fagus orientalis*)
Native to Asia Minor, Iran and Bulgaria, this species is of similar size to common beech (*Fagus sylvatica*) but has a more upright form, a fluted bole, darker grey bark and more pointed leaves.

Common beech (*Fagus sylvatica*)
This splendid tree, a native of Europe, has long (and with good reason) been called the 'Queen of the Forest'. Growing to over 40m (130ft) tall, with stately form and a huge domed crown, it is indeed a magnificent sight, with great silver-grey branches spreading from its sturdy buttressed bole up into the dense

Fern-leaved beech
Fagus sylvatica 'Heterophylla'
Has delicate, narrow, deeply
cut feathery leaves.

Dawyck beech
Fagus sylvatica 'Fastigiata'
Has a very narrow form
resembling that of
Lombardy poplar.

upper greenery and, on old open-grown trees, outwards to form a great circle of deep shade as much as 35m (120ft) in diameter. In the past, many trees were pollarded, resulting in a very short bole and many heavy branches, but when grown under expert forest management beech will provide long clean trunks of perfect timber, straight-grained and free from knots. The wood is pinkish buff, speckled with small, darker brown flecks, and even-grained. It is fairly hard, strong, easily worked and much in demand for furniture-making.

The slender, long-pointed, red-brown buds are 1.5–2cm (½–¾in) long, and the leaves emerge a lovely fresh green edged with delicate silver hairs; when mature they are obovate, up to 8 x 6cm (3 x 2½in), with well-marked parallel veins and slightly wavy edges.

Flowering occurs in late spring, just as the leaves expand; the male flowers are in the form of little golden tassels on long stalks, while the females are more upright, on shorter, stouter stalks, and with fine silver filaments tinged with pink and green.

Beech nuts, collectively known as 'mast', are triangular, short-pointed,

Copper beech
Fagus sylvatica 'Purpurea'
This has dark purple
leaves.

Weeping beech
Fagus sylvatica 'Pendula'
May be tall and narrow or
short and broad, but with
long pendulous shoots.

1.5–2cm (½–¾in) long, shining brown and usually develop two to each husk; the husks are four-lobed and covered with short prickles.

Common beech does well on chalk and limestone soils, where it is often the climax species. Its foliage is dense, casting a deep shade so that the ground beneath is usually bare of vegetation. It is a favourite species for avenues, large gardens and parks. Cultivars include:

'Cuprea' (copper beech), which is a common and conspicuous form of common beech, with coppery red leaves; there is a weeping variety.

'Fastigiata' (Dawyck or fastigiate beech), a remarkable variety, with narrowly ascending branches giving a form like Lombardy poplar (*Populus nigra* 'Italica', *see p.130*).

'Heterophylla' (fern-leaved beech), a handsome and graceful tree, with long leaves deeply cut into narrow pointed lobes giving a fern-like appearance.

'Pendula', an eye-catching tree with long weeping shoots.

'Purpurea' (purple beech), a common form, resembling copper beech ('Cuprea'), with dark purple leaves; there is a weeping variety.

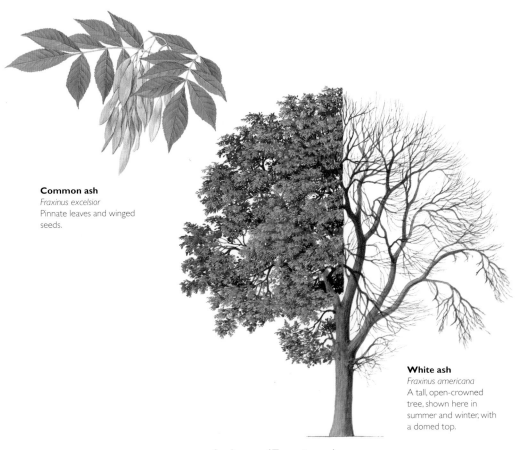

Common ash
Fraxinus excelsior
Pinnate leaves and winged
seeds.

White ash
Fraxinus americana
A tall, open-crowned
tree, shown here in
summer and winter, with
a domed top.

Ashes *(Fraxinus)*

There are some 60 species in this genus, nearly all in the northern hemisphere and mainly moderate- or large-sized trees. All have opposite buds, which in some are completely black; most have wind-pollinated flowers with petals, and pinnate leaves; and all have winged seeds. Several species yield excellent timber, valued for its special strength and resilience.

White ash
(Fraxinus americana)

This tree, which produces splendid timber, grows up to 40m (130ft) tall. The buds are dark brown, and the leaves, up to 40cm (16in), have seven to nine large leaflets (rarely more than seven). The flowers and fruit closely resemble those of common ash (*Fraxinus excelsior*).

Common ash *(Fraxinus excelsior)*

Native to Europe and Asia Minor, this is one of the largest and most important European broadleaved trees, growing up to 45m (150ft) tall, with girths up to 6m (20ft), and with a tall-domed open crown. It has very distinct jet black, squat, conic buds. The pinnate leaves are 16–35cm (6–14in) long, with 9 to 13 leaflets, each broadly lanceolate, acuminate and serrate. The tree shows extraor-

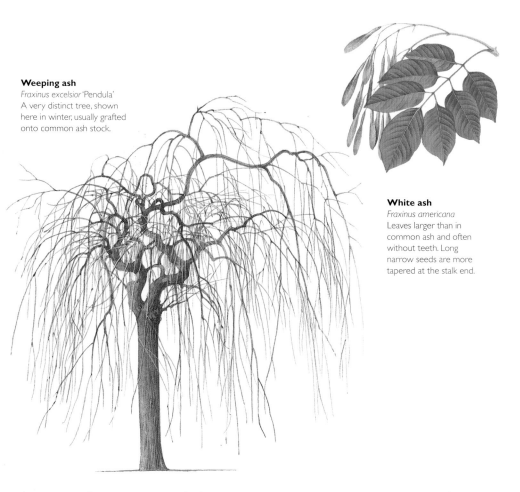

Weeping ash
Fraxinus excelsior 'Pendula'
A very distinct tree, shown
here in winter, usually grafted
onto common ash stock.

White ash
Fraxinus americana
Leaves larger than in
common ash and often
without teeth. Long
narrow seeds are more
tapered at the stalk end.

dinary sexual variation; not only do some trees have all female flowers, some all male and some mixed, but the flowers themselves are often mixed, even on the same twig; opening before the leaves, they are small and attractive, and occur in small feathery bunches, mixed purple, light yellow and green. The winged, strap-shaped seeds (often called 'keys'), about 3–4cm (1¼–1½in) long, on slender stalks 2–2.5cm (¾–1in) long, hang in clusters; pale green at first, then yellowish and finally brown, they often remain on the tree all winter.

The pale grey bark is smooth when young, but later develops a beautiful network of interwoven ridges and furrows.

Fraxinus excelsior has various cultivars, such as 'Pendula', which is a weeping type grafted on to common ash stock; and 'Monophylla', syn. 'Diversifolia', which is a remarkable freak with single simple leaves that are ovate-oblong and variably toothed.

Oregon ash *(Fraxinus latifolia* syn. *F. oregona)*

Another fine timber tree from western America, this is similar to white ash *(Fraxinus americana)* but not quite as large. It has unusually large side leaflets.

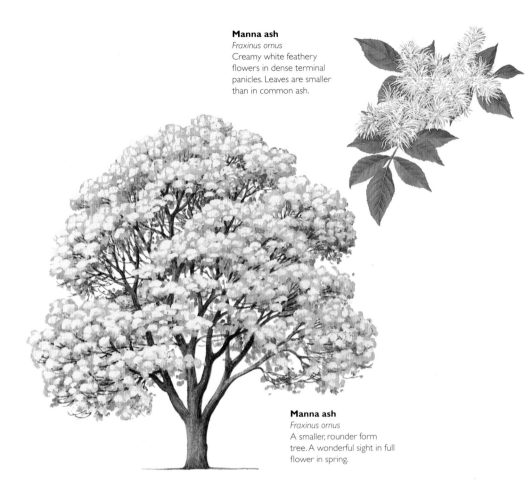

Manna ash
Fraxinus ornus
Creamy white feathery
flowers in dense terminal
panicles. Leaves are smaller
than in common ash.

Manna ash
Fraxinus ornus
A smaller, rounder form
tree. A wonderful sight in full
flower in spring.

Chinese flowering ash
(Fraxinus mariesii)
This is very similar to Manna or flowering ash (*Fraxinus ornus*) but the leaves have only three to five leaflets.

Black ash *(Fraxinus nigra)*
An important timber tree in western America, this grows almost as large as white ash (*Fraxinus americana*). It has dark brown buds; the leaves have 7 to 11 slender, pointed leaflets and turn pale yellow in the autumn.

Manna or flowering ash
(Fraxinus ornus)
This beautiful tree, up to 20m (70ft) tall, from southern Europe and western Asia, is a remarkable sight when covered in masses of fragrant creamy white flowers in late spring. 'Manna' sugar is obtained from the sap.

Red ash *(Fraxinus pennsylvanica)*
A fast-growing eastern North American tree, red ash is smaller than white ash (*Fraxinus americana*), with poorer quality timber, red-brown buds, downy shoots and large leaves.

The variety *lanceolata* (green ash) has much more slender leaves and leaflets, and no down on the shoots, unlike the species.

Maidenhair tree
Ginkgo biloba
Catkins and young leaves.

Maidenhair tree
Ginkgo biloba
Leaves change from yellow
in spring to green in
summer and gold in
autumn. Shown here in
spring and winter.

Maidenhair tree
Ginkgo biloba
The oval, plum-like fruits are
gold when ripe, on long stalks.

Maidenhair Tree (*Ginkgo biloba*)

The maidenhair tree is the sole survivor of an ancient family of trees, Ginkgoaceae.

Maidenhair Tree (*Ginkgo biloba*)
Native in China, the maidenhair tree is widely planted in all temperate regions as an ornamental tree growing to 30m (100ft) tall. It is deciduous, the leaves turning to a wonderful gold before falling in the autumn; and in the winter the very slender, rather gaunt tops of young trees, with their long bare leading shoots and short irregular side branches, are very distinctive, but with age they get broader with more rounded tops.

The foliage is very similar to the fronds of maidenhair fern. On emerging, the leaves are yellow, but turn green as they flatten out, becoming leathery, fan-shaped, with a cleft at the top, and variable in size, 6–10cm x 4–8cm (2½–4in x 1½–3in). They have conspicuous straight veins radiating from the base.

Nearly all the trees are male and have yellowish catkins 5–7cm (2–3in) long. On the very rare female trees, the small green ovoid flowers, 2–5cm (¾–2in) long, develop into fleshy oval-globular fruits, green at first but orange-yellow when ripe. The seeds are edible.

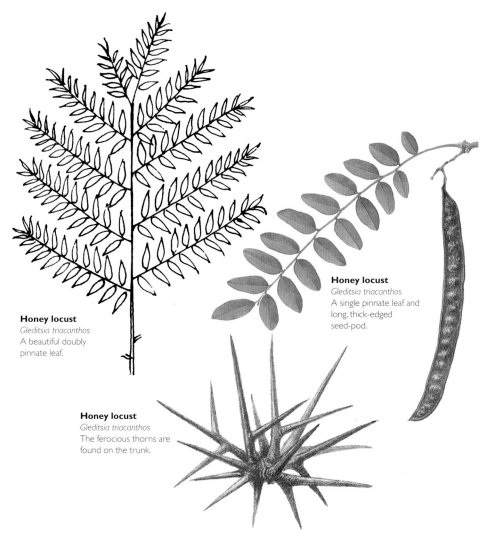

Honey locust
Gleditsia triacanthos
A beautiful doubly
pinnate leaf.

Honey locust
Gleditsia triacanthos
A single pinnate leaf and
long, thick-edged
seed-pod.

Honey locust
Gleditsia triacanthos
The ferocious thorns are
found on the trunk.

Honey Locust *(Gleditsia triacanthus)*

Gleditsia is a group of about a dozen species from North and South America, Africa and Asia, distinctive for the formidable thorns on their trunks and branches, large pinnate or bi-pinnate leaves, small flowers, and large seed-pods.

Honey locust *(Gleditsia triacanthos)*
Native to western USA, this is the best-known of the locusts. It is a large tree, up to 45m (150ft) tall, whose crown tends to be broadest at the top, with lovely fern-like leaves, 10–20cm (4–8in) long, with 14 to 32 oblong-lanceolate, glossy, bright green, shallowly toothed leaflets, 1.5–4cm (½–1½in) long and turning gold in autumn. The buds are protected by spines and large thorns, up to 25cm (10in) long, which also protect the branches and trunk; the greenish flowers are tiny. The pods are large, 20–40cm x 2–3cm (8–16in x ¾–1¼in), twisted, and yellow-green ripening to brown.

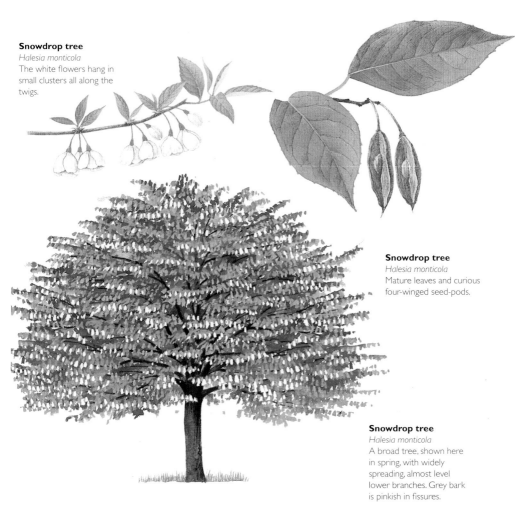

Snowdrop tree
Halesia monticola
The white flowers hang in small clusters all along the twigs.

Snowdrop tree
Halesia monticola
Mature leaves and curious four-winged seed-pods.

Snowdrop tree
Halesia monticola
A broad tree, shown here in spring, with widely spreading, almost level lower branches. Grey bark is pinkish in fissures.

Snowdrop Tree (*Halesia monticola*)

Snowdrop trees are among the few members of the storax family (Styracaceae) that grow to tree size. They are useful in providing the gardener with a range of fine trees that thrive in a lime-free soil.

Snowdrop or silverbell tree (*Halesia monticola*)

Quite a large, broadly conic tree up to 30m (100ft) tall, from the mountain areas of southeastern USA, bearing heavy crops of pendulous white flowers up to 3cm (1¼in) long, on stalks 2cm (¾in) long, just as the leaves are flushing in late spring. The bluntly jointed leaves are finely serrated, oblong-ovate, with conspicuous impressed veins.

The fruits are almost pear shaped, up to 5cm (2in) long, with four narrow wings. They are pale green at first, but finally turn brown. The bark is dark grey with pinkish fissures.

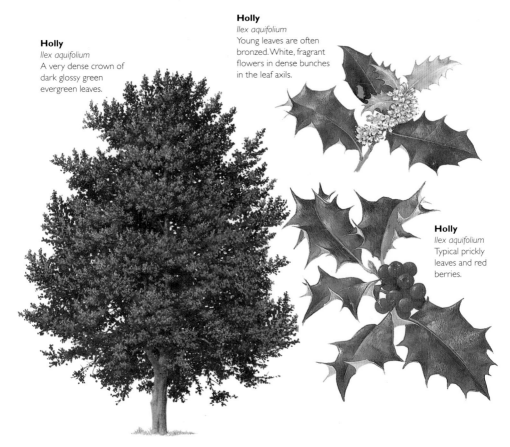

Holly
Ilex aquifolium
A very dense crown of
dark glossy green
evergreen leaves.

Holly
Ilex aquifolium
Young leaves are often
bronzed. White, fragrant
flowers in dense bunches
in the leaf axils.

Holly
Ilex aquifolium
Typical prickly
leaves and red
berries.

Holly *(Ilex aquifolium)*

Holly is one of the few evergreen broadleaved trees that thrive in northern Europe.

Holly *(Ilex aquifolium)*

Holly's glossy, twisted leaves, dark green above and paler below, often bear characteristic prickles along their edges. In the typical wild form, the upper leaves are oval and pointed, but spineless. Garden strains are sometimes spiny right to the top, others spineless to the bottom. There are some striking decorative cultivars, variegated with silver or gold on their leaves, or even red, white and green on the same leaf. The waxy surface of the foliage checks water loss.

Every holly tree is either wholly male or wholly female. The female produces bright red or yellow berries around midwinter. When hollies flower, in late spring, they open clusters of short-stalked blossoms along their outer twigs. The four petals of each flower have a waxy surface and are white, with purple tips. Male flowers have four stamens with yellow anthers, while female flowers develop a squat, oval green pistil. The fruit, which ripens late in autumn, is a scarlet berry, holding four hard brown seeds. Holly bark is smooth and grey.

Butternut
Juglans cinerea
Even larger leaves than black walnut. Husks usually ribbed and nuts in groups of three to seven, small, oily and very sweet.

Walnuts *(Juglans)*

There is something aristocratic about a walnut tree; it offers only the very best both in timber and delicious nuts. The Latin name *Juglans* means the nut of Jove or Jupiter and the name walnut is derived from the old English words meaning 'foreign nut'.

The 15 or so different species of walnut together show a wide distribution from North and South America, China and Japan across to northern Asia and all over Europe.

Japanese walnut *(Juglans ailantifolia)*
This Japanese species is scattered through Europe and the USA. It is a smaller tree than the other walnuts — up to 15m (50ft) — but has huge leaves up to 1m (3ft) long with 11 to 12 leaflets, and the male catkins are up to 30cm (12in) long. A close relation, *Juglans hindsii*, is a favourite tree in California.

Butternut *(Juglans cinerea)*
This American species has sweet and oily nuts and leaves even larger than those of the black walnut (*Juglans nigra*) — up to 80cm (32in) or more in length.

Arizona walnut *(Juglans major)*
Another American species, this is found in the canyons of the southwestern United States and northwestern Mexico.

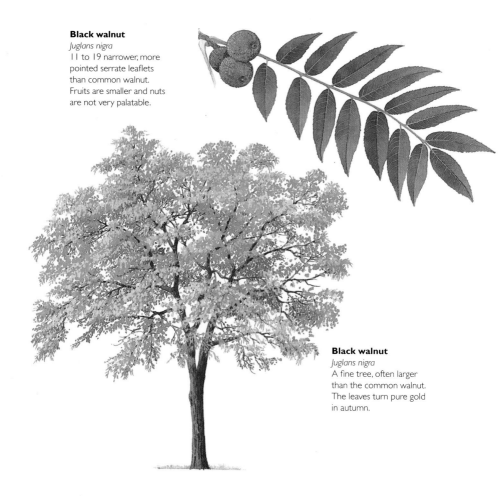

Black walnut
Juglans nigra
11 to 19 narrower, more
pointed serrate leaflets
than common walnut.
Fruits are smaller and nuts
are not very palatable.

Black walnut
Juglans nigra
A fine tree, often larger
than the common walnut.
The leaves turn pure gold
in autumn.

Black Walnut (*Juglans nigra*)

An American tree, now introduced into
many other countries, the black walnut
is hardier, taller (up to 33m/108ft) and
less spreading than the common walnut
(*Juglans regia*), and has larger leaves
(30–50cm/12–20in) with many more
leaflets (11 to 23). The nuts are much
inferior to those of the common walnut.

There is a fine cut-leaved cultivar
called 'Laciniata'. Hybrids have been
made between common walnut and
black walnut, under the general name of
Juglans x *intermedia*, but most of them
have inferior nuts.

Common or English walnut
(*Juglans regia*)

This is the best-known species, a broad-
crowned tree up to 23m (77ft) in height,
with light grey, rugged bark, fissured
between fairly broad plates. In common
with all the walnuts, it has the special
characteristic of air-pockets in the pith,
which can be seen clearly if a twig is split
open. This characteristic distinguishes
the walnut from the otherwise similar
hickory (*Carya*), which has a solid pith.

New growth is easily damaged by
frost, but fortunately spring flushing is
very late, the flowers and leaves not

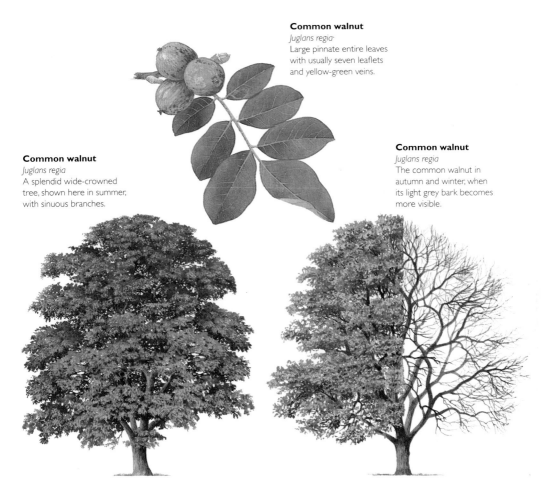

Common walnut
Juglans regia·
Large pinnate entire leaves
with usually seven leaflets
and yellow-green veins.

Common walnut
Juglans regia
A splendid wide-crowned
tree, shown here in summer,
with sinuous branches.

Common walnut
Juglans regia
The common walnut in
autumn and winter, when
its light grey bark becomes
more visible.

breaking out until late spring or early summer; when the foliage is young it is of a beautiful reddish brown colour, which does not give way to green until the large alternate pinnate leaves, 20–40cm (8–16in) long with three to nine (usually seven) smooth-edged leaflets, are well expanded. The mature leaves smell acrid when crushed and the sap from them stains the hands.

The male catkins of the common walnut are plump, 5–8cm (2–3in) long, reddish at first but turning yellowish green before they fall, while the female flowers are very small, yellow-green, and found in small clusters of two to five at the end of some of the younger twigs.

The delicious nuts are large, approximately 3–5cm (1¼–2in) in diameter, and are always much in demand for cookery. The finest nuts come from the French special clones such as the 'Franquette' cultivar, and there is a cut-leaved cultivar of common walnut called 'Laciniata'.

Walnut timber, in varying shades of brown colour, and patterned with streaks and curves of both lighter and darker shades, is strong, tough, elastic and highly valued, particularly for furniture and gun-butts.

Common juniper
Juniperus communis
A small tree preferring limestone soils and amazingly variable in shape. Tall narrow type shown here. Beautiful blue-grey foliage.

Chinese juniper
Juniperus chinensis
Has mixed juvenile and mature foliage.

Junipers *(Juniperus)*

A genus with over 50 species, as well as endless cultivated varieties, ranging widely over the northern hemisphere from the Arctic Circle to Mexico and from Britain to the Himalayas, China and Japan. Their special features include very small round flowers, small berry-like cones, leaves of two distinct types, some needle-like, others with small overlapping appressed scales (in some species both types on the same twig), a pungent aromatic scent to the bruised foliage, and an ability to survive on both alkaline and acid soils and either dry or wet situations.

Chinese juniper *(Juniperus chinensis)*
This tree grows up to 20m (70ft) in height, and is native in China and Japan. It is very similar in most respects to the pencil cedar *(Juniperus virginiana)* but has slightly larger leaf scales and cones, and juvenile leaves which tend to be near the base of the shoots instead of at the tips. There are many cultivars available, one of the best of which is 'Aurea', a beautiful narrow-form golden tree.

Common juniper
(Juniperus communis)
This bush or small tree, seldom as tall as 5m (15ft), though in rare cases up to

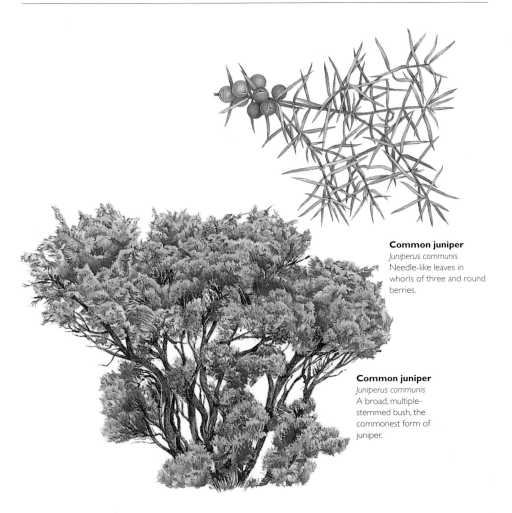

Common juniper
Juniperus communis
Needle-like leaves in
whorls of three and round
berries.

Common juniper
Juniperus communis
A broad, multiple-
stemmed bush, the
commonest form of
juniper.

15m (50ft), has a wide distribution from northern Europe to Asia, the Himalayas, the Caucasus, Canada and North America. It is unusual as it favours either very alkaline soils, such as chalk downland, or very acid soils, such as boggy heathland.

The sharply pointed acicular leaves, up to 1cm (½in) long, in whorls of three, are grey-green on the outer surface but with a broad white band on the inside.

Male flowers are tiny yellow globes, and occur on separate trees from equally small greenish female flowers. The globular berries, approximately 7mm (¼in), take as long as two years to ripen. They are green at first, then blue-bloomed and finally black. An aromatic oil used for medical purposes is distilled from the unripe berries, and the ripe ones are crushed for flavouring gin. The bark is greyish and flakes off in long fibrous strips. There are many cultivars available, such as the blue-green tall slim columnar 'Hibernica' and the dwarf bushy 'Compressa'.

Syrian juniper *(Juniperus drupacea)*
A fine, quite distinct species from Greece, Asia Minor and Syria, narrowly conic or columnar in form and up to 17m (56ft) in height, this tree has the longest

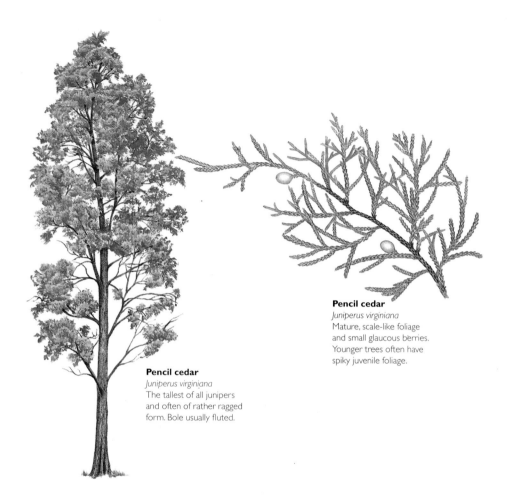

Pencil cedar
Juniperus virginiana
Mature, scale-like foliage
and small glaucous berries.
Younger trees often have
spiky juvenile foliage.

Pencil cedar
Juniperus virginiana
The tallest of all junipers
and often of rather ragged
form. Bole usually fluted.

spiny sharp-pointed needles of any juniper, each 1.5–2.5cm (½–1in) long, shining green on the outer surface, with two silver bands on the inner side. The berry is the largest of the genus — up to 2.5cm (1in) in diameter.

Western juniper

(Juniperus occidentalis)

This is closely allied to the Utah species *(Juniperus osteosperma)*, but is much larger — up to 20m (70ft).

Utah juniper

(Juniperus osteosperma syn. *J. utahensis)*

This desert species, with short, heavily

gnarled trunks, is a conspicuous feature of high altitude, arid regions between the Sierra Nevada and the Rocky Mountains.

Pencil cedar

(Juniperus virginiana)

A native of Canada and eastern USA, this is the tallest species, sometimes exceeding 30m (100ft). The trunk is usually fluted and the reddish brown bark peels off in narrow strips. It is a narrowly conic tree with mainly small scale-like leaves, but juvenile needle-type foliage may be found on the ends of some twigs. The small berry-like cones are green at first but develop a silvery blue bloom later.

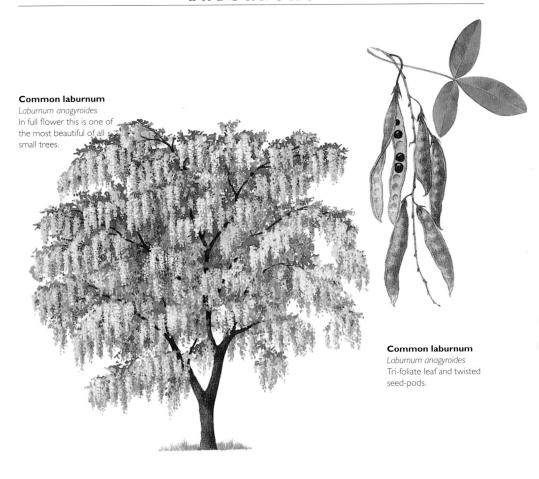

Common laburnum
Laburnum anagyroides
In full flower this is one of the most beautiful of all small trees.

Common laburnum
Laburnum anagyroides
Tri-foliate leaf and twisted seed-pods.

Laburnums *(Laburnum)*

This genus of three species, two native to central and southern Europe and the other to Greece and Asia Minor, all have deciduous, tri-foliate, alternate leaves, yellow flowers in long racemes, and seeds in clusters of small pods. The leaves and seeds are poisonous.

Scotch laburnum *(Laburnum alpinum)*
A European species only differing from common laburnum *(Laburnum anagyroides)* in having less hairy and larger leaves, 8–13cm (3–5in) long, flowers more widely spaced on longer racemes, 20–35cm (8–14in), and seed-pods with a distinct wing along the upper edge.

Common laburnum or golden rain
(Laburnum anagyroides syn. *L. vulgare)*
This is one of the most widely used ornamental trees, particularly in Europe. It is a striking sight, covered with its golden rain of pendulous bright yellow flowers, each raceme 15–25cm (6–10in) long. The slender leaflets, 5–8cm (2–3in) long, are grey-green above, silky and silvery on the underside. After a few years, the attractive trunk bark is shiny, pale brown with fine fissures. If allowed to grow naturally, laburnums will reach about 12m (40ft), with ascending arching branches.

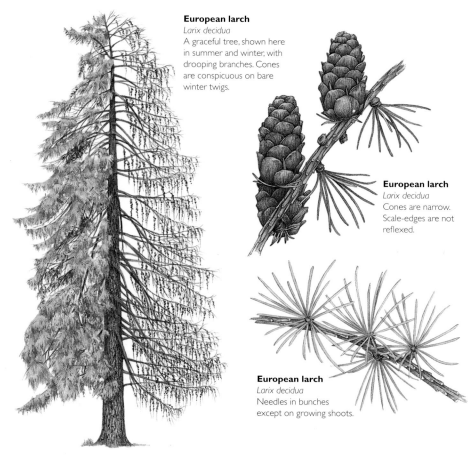

European larch
Larix decidua
A graceful tree, shown here
in summer and winter, with
drooping branches. Cones
are conspicuous on bare
winter twigs.

European larch
Larix decidua
Cones are narrow.
Scale-edges are not
reflexed.

European larch
Larix decidua
Needles in bunches
except on growing shoots.

Larches *(Larix)*

The larches are a small family, only
about a dozen species, and are
among the very few deciduous conifers.
In spring they burst into vivid green earlier than most trees; in autumn the
leaves turn gold; in winter the bare twigs
stand out, from pale yellow to dark red-
brown, according to species.

A special feature of the larches is the
arrangement of their needles: on long
shoots they are set singly, spirally all
along the twig, but on the short spur-like
shoots, and on older woods, they are
borne in whorls, of from 15 to 40 in each
tuft, as in cedars (*Cedrus*).

European larch
(*Larix decidua* syn. *L. europaea*)
Native to south and central Europe, with
particularly straight and vigorous forms
in the Sudeten and the plains of Poland,
also in Russia and Siberia where it
merges into the species *Larix sibirica*
(this is a smaller tree with slender needles that flush too early when planted
further south and get caught by spring
frosts). European larch is a rapid grower,
often having annual shoots of 1m (3ft) or
more, and reaches up to 50m (160ft),
with diameters up to 2m (6ft). The bright
green needles are 2–4cm (¾–1½in) long,

88

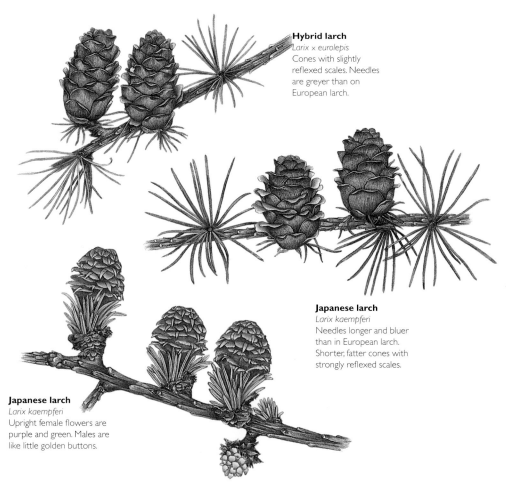

Hybrid larch
Larix × eurolepis
Cones with slightly reflexed scales. Needles are greyer than on European larch.

Japanese larch
Larix kaempferi
Needles longer and bluer than in European larch. Shorter, fatter cones with strongly reflexed scales.

Japanese larch
Larix kaempferi
Upright female flowers are purple and green. Males are like little golden buttons.

the winter twigs pale straw-coloured or pinkish fawn, and the cones are oblong-ovoid, narrower towards the top, 2.5–4cm (1–1½in) long x 2–2.5cm (¾–1in) broad, scales rounded and without any curving back of the tips. Bark on old trunks is quite deeply fissured.

Hybrid or Dunkeld larch
(Larix × eurolepis)

This is a cross between the European and Japanese larches (*Larix decidua* and *L. kaempferi*), and has features intermediate between the two. On good sites its growth is superior to both, often making leading shoots from 1–2m (3–6ft).

Japanese larch
(Larix kaempferi syn. L. leptolepis)

This tree is similar to the European larch (*Larix decidua*) but has the following distinctions: the cones are shorter (2–3cm/¾–1¼in), more rounded and with strongly reflexed edges to the scales; the winter twigs are much darker and usually reddish brown; the needles are longer, a little wider and more bluish green; the leading shoots are often slightly wavy; and the bark is less deeply fissured.

On poor soils, or very exposed sites, this species will succeed better than will the European larch.

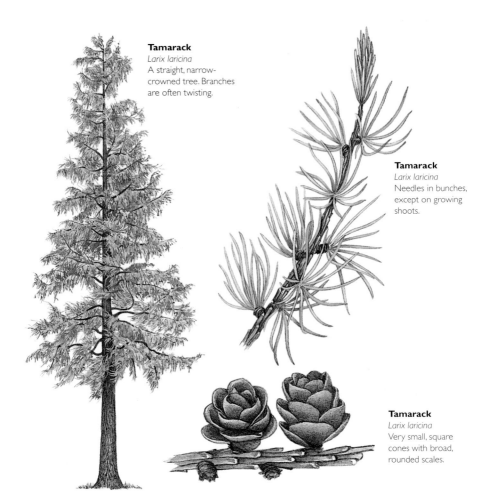

Tamarack
Larix laricina
A straight, narrow-crowned tree. Branches are often twisting.

Tamarack
Larix laricina
Needles in bunches, except on growing shoots.

Tamarack
Larix laricina
Very small, square cones with broad, rounded scales.

Tamarack or American larch

(Larix laricina)

This remarkable and extremely hardy tree has the widest natural range of any American conifer, extending from the Yukon right along the northern limit of tree growth to Newfoundland and Labrador, with its southern boundary from British Columbia to Pennsylvania. It will tolerate extremely low temperatures, swampy ground, low rainfall and elevations from sea level to 1,200m (3,936ft). On average, it grows to about 22m (75ft) but on the best sites it may reach 35m (120ft). The needles are simi-

lar to those of the European larch (*Larix decidua*), but slightly smaller; the cones of the tamarack are much smaller, up to 2 x 1.5cm (¾ x ½in).

Western larch *(Larix occidentalis)*

This is the other main larch in America. It is a much larger tree than the tamarack, growing up to 60m (200ft), but with only a small native range in the upper Columbia River Basin. It lives to a great age — up to about 900 years. The needles are like those of the European larch (*Larix decidua*) but the cones are larger, 3–6cm (1¼–2½in) long, with curved, pointed projecting bracts.

Sweet bay
Laurus nobilis
A dense bush or small tree, broadly pyramidal and often with several stems, shown here in summer.

Sweet bay
Laurus nobilis
The leathery, crinkly edged leaves are very aromatic.

Sweet bay
Laurus nobilis
Berries are green, turning to shining black.

Sweet Bay *(Laurus nobilis)*

Laurus nobilis is the only true laurel. Both of the common so-called laurels (cherry laurel and Portugal laurel) are in fact members of the great *Prunus* genus, and are dealt with under that heading (*see pp.131–140*).

Sweet bay, bay tree or poet's laurel (*Laurus nobilis*)

Native to the Mediterranean, and growing to about 18m (60ft), this is the famous species whose leaves were used to crown the heroes of olden times. Today, the leaves of sweet bay are still gathered for flavouring savoury dishes and for scenting linen in drawers and cupboards with their characteristic aroma.

The dark, evergreen, leathery lanceolate leaves are finely toothed and up to 10 x 3cm (4 x 1¼in), often with red basal veins visible.

The pale yellow flowers, about 1cm (½in) across, are produced in small umbels at the base of the leaves, the sexes being on separate trees.

The fruit is a green, shiny, slightly oval berry, about 1cm (½in) across, turning black when ripe. On young trees, the blackish grey bark is fairly smooth, but as the tree ages it gradually becomes wrinkled and cracked.

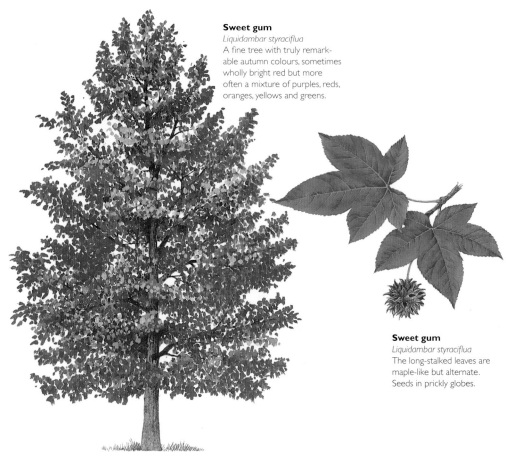

Sweet gum
Liquidambar styraciflua
A fine tree with truly remarkable autumn colours, sometimes
wholly bright red but more
often a mixture of purples, reds,
oranges, yellows and greens.

Sweet gum
Liquidambar styraciflua
The long-stalked leaves are
maple-like but alternate.
Seeds in prickly globes.

Sweet Gums *(Liquidambar)*

Sweet gums are so called because they exude a fragrant yellow resinous gum. Of the six species in this little group, only three are commonly met with.

Chinese sweet gum
(Liquidambar formosana)
This tree grows to about 40m (130ft). It has hairy young shoots and leaves, and a heavily buttressed trunk.

Oriental sweet gum
(Liquidambar orientalis)
From Asia Minor, this tree grows to 30m (100ft), with orange-brown flaking bark and five-lobed, hairless leaves on long stalks. It has attractive autumn colours.

Sweet gum *(Liquidambar styraciflua)*
This tree can reach 40m (130ft) tall and 2m (6ft) in diameter. The leaves, 10–15cm (4–6in) long, with three to seven lobes, are like maple leaves but are alternate on the twigs; the small yellow-ish green flowers are inconspicuous, in little round clusters, and the fruits are burr-like, in roundish clusters, 2–3cm (¾–1¼in) across when fully developed, hanging on stalks about 4–5cm (1½–2in) long, either singly or several together. The rough grey bark is much fissured between heavy ridges. This is one of the finest of all trees for autumn colours.

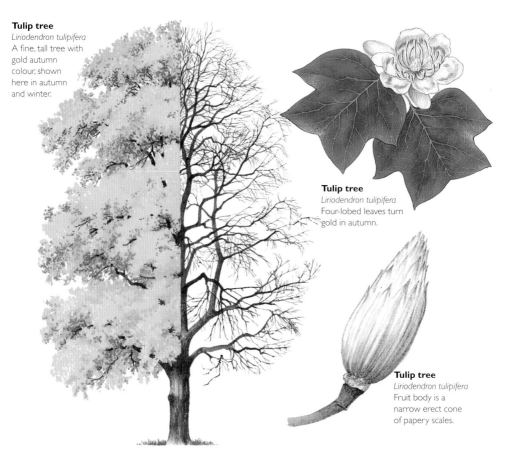

Tulip tree
Liriodendron tulipifera
A fine, tall tree with gold autumn colour, shown here in autumn and winter.

Tulip tree
Liriodendron tulipifera
Four-lobed leaves turn gold in autumn.

Tulip tree
Liriodendron tulipifera
Fruit body is a narrow erect cone of papery scales.

Tulip Trees (*Liriodendron*)

There are only two species of tulip tree; the best known, *Liriodendron tulipifera*, is native to North America.

Chinese tulip tree
(*Liriodendron chinensis*)

This smaller species only grows to about 20m (70ft), with more deeply waisted leaves and rather smaller but very similar flowers. The fruit is slightly longer.

Tulip tree (*Liriodendron tulipifera*)

This fine ornamental tree grows to a height of 57m (190ft), with a tall, many-domed crown and heavy lower branches. The bark is much-fissured when mature, light orange-brown, and often with burrs.

The buds, about 1cm (½in) long, are brown in colour, bloomed with lilac, and flattened with curved tips. The unique leaves are saddle-shaped, four-lobed and truncated at the ends, up to 15 x 20cm (6 x 8in); in autumn they are bright gold, turning sometimes to rich brown. The flowers appear in early summer (though not usually for the first 15 to 20 years), tulip-shaped at first, then widening out; they have six petals, pale greenish yellow with orange markings near the base and many fleshy yellow stamens. The fruit is a papery, erect, narrow-pointed cone, the seeds have long narrow wings.

Cucumber tree
Magnolia acuminata
Erect purple-red fruits and
large pointed leaves.

Cucumber tree
Magnolia acuminata
Large, upright-form tree.
Foliage hides the greenish
yellow flowers.

Magnolias *(Magnolia)*

This large group of about 40 species, mostly from America, East Asia and the Himalayas, includes some of the finest flowering trees; they may be evergreen or deciduous, and have large solitary terminal flowers and cone-like fruits and buds, each with a single scale.

Cucumber tree *(Magnolia acuminata)*
The special feature of this deciduous American tree, which reaches 30m (100ft) tall, is its curious fruit, resembling short upright cucumbers, about 8 x 4cm (3 x 1½in), green at first but turning through pink to red. The greenish yellow flowers, about 10cm (4in) across, are not very noticeable among the large, pointed, broadly elliptic glossy green leaves, about 20 x 12cm (8 x 5in).

Chinese evergreen magnolia
(Magnolia delavayi)
This evergreen species is from southwest China and grows to about 15m (50ft) tall. It has dull, grey-green, very wide leaves, about 22 x 16cm (9 x 6in), and large fruits, up to 14cm (5½in) long. The flowers resemble those of southern magnolia *(Magnolia grandiflora)*, but they are not quite as large, and the bark of Chinese evergreen magnolia is lighter coloured and of a more corky consistency.

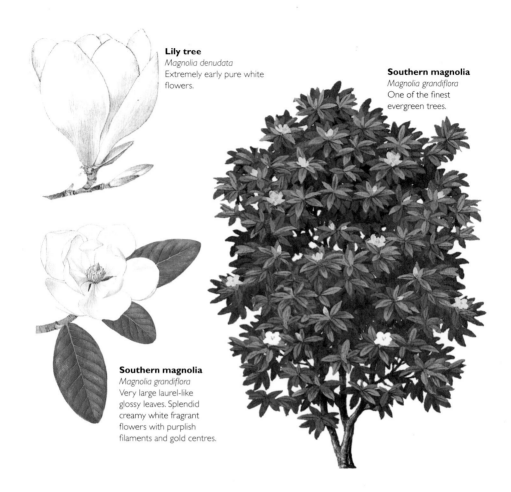

Lily tree
Magnolia denudata
Extremely early pure white flowers.

Southern magnolia
Magnolia grandiflora
One of the finest evergreen trees.

Southern magnolia
Magnolia grandiflora
Very large laurel-like glossy leaves. Splendid creamy white fragrant flowers with purplish filaments and gold centres.

Lily tree or Yulan

(Magnolia denudata syn. *M. conspicua)*
This beautiful Chinese species, up to 15m (50ft) tall, has pure white flowers that open even earlier than those of Japanese magnolia (*Magnolia stellata*) and are often spoilt by frost. A special feature is its winter buds, which are covered with shaggy hairs.

Southern, laurel or bull bay magnolia

(Magnolia grandiflora)
This species from southeastern USA is one of the finest of all flowering evergreen trees, growing up to 24m (79ft) tall with large, rich, green, glossy leather

leaves up to 24 x 12cm (10 x 5in), but normally about 15 x 7cm (6 x 3in). The fragrant creamy white flowers, 18–25cm (7–10in) across, have six thick petals and flower from midsummer to mid-autumn. The fruits are narrowly ovoid, about 6 x 3cm (2½ x 1¼in), with purple-green pubescent scales; the bark is dark greyish green with only shallow fissures. In cold areas it is best against a warm wall.

Large-leafed cucumber tree

(Magnolia macrophylla)
This American species is similar to, though smaller than the cucumber tree (*Magnolia acuminata*), with enormous

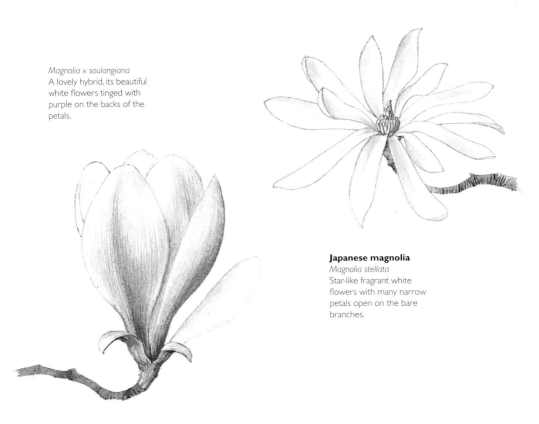

Magnolia × soulangiana
A lovely hybrid, its beautiful white flowers tinged with purple on the backs of the petals.

Japanese magnolia
Magnolia stellata
Star-like fragrant white flowers with many narrow petals open on the bare branches.

blunt-pointed, bright green auricled leaves, 20–70cm (8–28in) long x 15–38cm (6–15in) wide, and larger creamy white flowers, which usually grow up to 20cm (8in) across.

Magnolia × soulangiana

This hybrid between *Magnolia denudata* and *M. obovata* is one of the most popular magnolias. Its growth is vigorous, up to 8m (25ft) high, and it has very broad, tulip-shaped white, rose-backed flowers starting on bare branches but persisting until after the leaves are out. It flowers a little later and is therefore less often frost damaged than some other magnolias.

There are many special clones of this excellent species, such as 'Rustica rubra', with rich red flowers, and 'Lennei', with larger leaves and purple-backed flowers.

Japanese magnolia (*Magnolia stellata*)

With its masses of pure white fragrant flowers on bare branches in early spring, this small rounded tree, up to 2m (6ft) tall, is one of the best loved of all magnolias. Each flower has from 12 to 18 narrow petals, about 4–5cm (1½–2in) long. It is liable to frost damage owing to its early flowering.

The cultivar 'Rosea' has beautiful pinkish purple tinged petals.

American crab apple
Malus coronaria
Fine, large, beautifully
scented pink-white
flowers.

Japanese crab apple
Malus floribunda
A broad-crowned tree,
with masses of red buds
opening to pink flowers.

Crab Apples *(Malus)*

There are about 30 species of wild apple trees in the north temperate regions and many hundreds of hybrids and cultivars, which have been raised from them either for fruit or ornament. Here we shall not consider the huge fruit production aspect, but confine ourselves to a few of the original crab apples and some of their most important progeny, which together are second only to cherries in popularity for ornamental planting the world over.

Siberian crab apple *(Malus baccata)*
A common, very hardy native tree in Siberia, Manchuria and northern China, this grows up to 10m (30ft) tall with a tendency to pendulous branches and rather narrow leaves, up to 6 x 2.5cm (2½ x 1in), white flowers on slender stalks, and bright red fruit.

Siberian crab has yielded large numbers of hybrids and cultivars, providing a wonderful range of ornamental trees, much used in the gardens of the world. Examples are 'Lemoinei', with crimson-purple flowers; 'Eleyi', with bright red-purple flowers; 'Robusta', with bright scarlet, cherry-like fruits; and 'Golden Hornet', with bright yellow fruits — the last two cultivars both retain their fruits for months, well past leaf-fall.

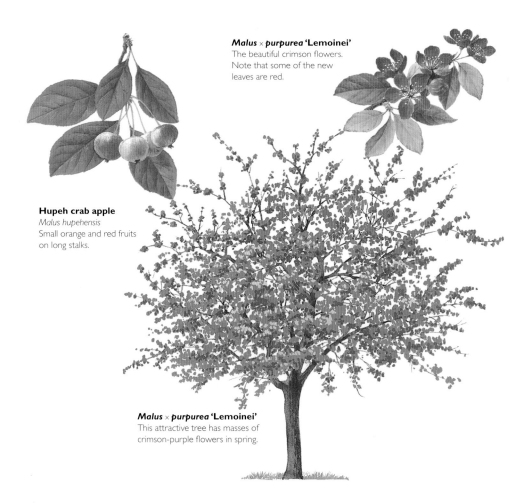

Malus × purpurea 'Lemoinei'
The beautiful crimson flowers.
Note that some of the new
leaves are red.

Hupeh crab apple
Malus hupehensis
Small orange and red fruits
on long stalks.

Malus × purpurea 'Lemoinei'
This attractive tree has masses of
crimson-purple flowers in spring.

American or sweet crab apple
(Malus coronaria)
Native to eastern North America, this tree has large, beautifully scented pink and white flowers on long stalks and yellowish green round fruits. The leaves, 5–14cm (2–5½in), colour well in autumn.

Japanese crab apple *(Malus floribunda)*
One of the most beautiful Japanese trees, not very tall with arching branches, prolific rosy red flowers and either yellow or red small fruits.

Hupeh or tea crab apple
(Malus hupehensis)
This is a Chinese species with stiff ascending branches, small abundant bunches of pink and white flowers, and small orange and red fruits. Sometimes used in China as a substitute for tea.

Sikkim crab apple *(Malus sikkimensis)*
This low, bushy Himalayan tree has rigid branching spurs on the trunk at the base of the branches, flowers that are pink in bud, white when out, and abundant very small, pear-shaped dark red fruits.

Chinese crab apple *(Malus spectabilis)*
A fine tree from north China, this has large, slightly double, bright rosy-pink flowers, up to 5cm (2in) across, turning pale pink later, and small yellow fruits.

European crab apple
Malus sylvestris
A small, very dense crown, shown here in summer and winter, with twisting branches.

European crab apple
Malus sylvestris
Flowers are white and pink. Leaves are deep green above, whitish green beneath.

European crab apple
Malus sylvestris 'John Downie'
Masses of white flowers and beautiful orange and red fruits.

European crab apple

(Malus sylvestris syn. *M. pumila)*
Native to Europe and southwestern Asia, this is the progenitor of the domestic apple orchard, but it took generations of skilled work to transform its small sour fruit, really only suitable for making a special jelly, into sweeter and much larger apples.

This original crab apple has a bushy form, with dense twisting branches, and is seldom more than 8m (26ft) high. It often has quite thorny deep green leaves, up to 6 x 4cm (2½ x 1½in), which are fairly shiny above, whitish green and

pubescent beneath. The leaves are variable in shape, and may be ovate or elliptic, with pointed or fairly round ends. The flowers are small and mainly white, sometimes with a pink tinge, especially on the buds. The fruit is nearly round, about 2.5 x 3cm (1 x 1¼in), yellow with some red markings. The bark of the European crab is grey-brown in colour, and fissured into irregular small plates.

The main ornamental varieties have differences in the colour of the fruits rather than of the flowers. 'John Downie' is well known for its white flowers and quite large orange red fruits.

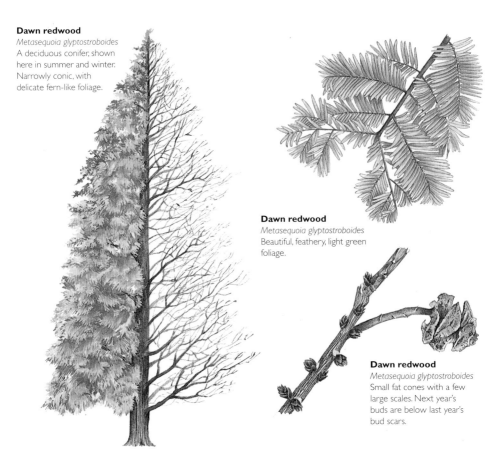

Dawn redwood
Metasequoia glyptostroboides
A deciduous conifer, shown
here in summer and winter.
Narrowly conic, with
delicate fern-like foliage.

Dawn redwood
Metasequoia glyptostroboides
Beautiful, feathery, light green
foliage.

Dawn redwood
Metasequoia glyptostroboides
Small fat cones with a few
large scales. Next year's
buds are below last year's
bud scars.

Dawn Redwood *(Metasequoia glyptostroboides)*

Genus of one species, which was thought to be extinct until 1941, when it was discovered growing in southwest China. It is now widely planted in many countries as an ornamental tree, and is of added interest because it is one of the few deciduous conifers.

Dawn redwood
(Metasequoia glyptostroboides)
Characterized by its narrowly conic form, ascending branches and rapid early growth, the dawn redwood reaches a height of at least 35m (120ft), possibly more on good sites. It strongly resembles the swamp cypress (*Taxodium dis-*

tichum). A unique feature is that the buds of the dawn redwood, which are opposite and not alternate as in swamp cypress, appear below the twigs, not in the axils as is normal. Its beautiful green foliage has longer, softer leaves (2–4cm/¾–1½in) than those of swamp cypress.

The flowers are tiny and similar to those of swamp cypress, while the cones, 1.5–2.5cm (½–1in), are round to ovoid with a short pointed tip, have only a few relatively large scales, and are on long stalks. On older trees, the trunk often becomes deeply fluted and buttressed and the bark comes away in strips.

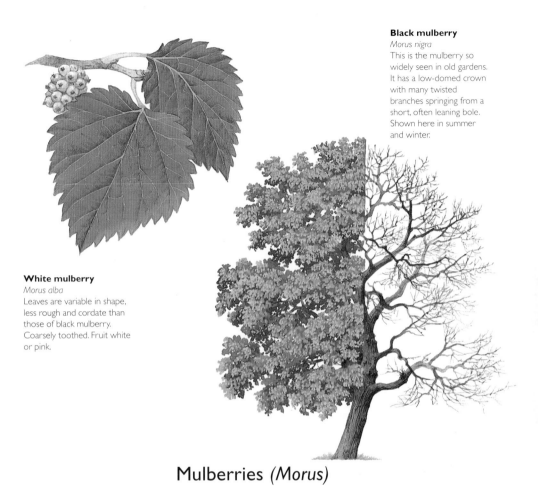

Black mulberry
Morus nigra
This is the mulberry so widely seen in old gardens. It has a low-domed crown with many twisted branches springing from a short, often leaning bole. Shown here in summer and winter.

White mulberry
Morus alba
Leaves are variable in shape, less rough and cordate than those of black mulberry. Coarsely toothed. Fruit white or pink.

Mulberries *(Morus)*

The mulberries belong to the Moraceae, a huge family with over a thousand species, growing mainly in the tropics, and having the special characteristic of milky sap; figs are one of the best-known members of this group.

There are about a dozen true mulberries (*Morus*) native to China, the USA, Mexico, Iran and Russia; they are usually associated with the silk industry because the worms feed on their leaves.

White mulberry *(Morus alba)*
This is a narrower, taller, faster-growing tree, up to 18m (60ft) high, with unusually variable leaves, sometimes like black mulberry (*Morus nigra*) but often with large, rounded, irregular lobes. Its pinkish white fruits are not as palatable as those of the black mulberry, but the leaves are the best for feeding silkworms, although in France black mulberries were often used for that purpose.

Russian mulberry *(Morus antarctica)*
The hardiest of the mulberries, this has even smaller leaves than the Mexican variety (*Morus microphylla*).

Mexican mulberry *(Morus microphylla)*
Also native to the USA and Mexico, this mulberry has small leaves, only 5–7cm (2–3in) long.

Black mulberry
Morus nigra
Broadly ovate, coarsely toothed, deeply cordate leaves on short stalks. Fruits green at first, red when ripe and dark purple when they fall in late summer.

Red mulberry
Morus rubra
Rounded, downy leaves, turning bright yellow in autumn. Red fruit.

Black mulberry *(Morus nigra)*

Originally from Iran, this is the most widely planted mulberry. It has been cultivated for thousands of years and is a fashionable feature of large old gardens. Its cordate, hairy, crenate leaves, 8–14cm (3–5½in) long, with stout stalks, are roughly heart-shaped but have a distinct point; deep green above, much paler beneath, they turn pale gold in autumn. The small clusters of pale greenish flowers are only about 1cm (⅓in) long and the well-known fruits, rather like rough raspberries, are rather acid when red but become sweeter as they turn through dark crimson to almost black. The tree has a broad rounded crown, seldom more than 12m (40ft) high, and quickly develops an old, gnarled appearance, often with burrs and bosses on the trunk and larger branches; the bark is pinkish brown and finely fissured.

Red mulberry *(Morus rubra)*

This species from the USA is the largest of all the mulberry trees, growing up to 25m (80ft), with a diameter up to 1.5m (5ft). It has a dense rounded crown, spreading branches and brown scaly bark. The fruits are mainly fed to animals and poultry.

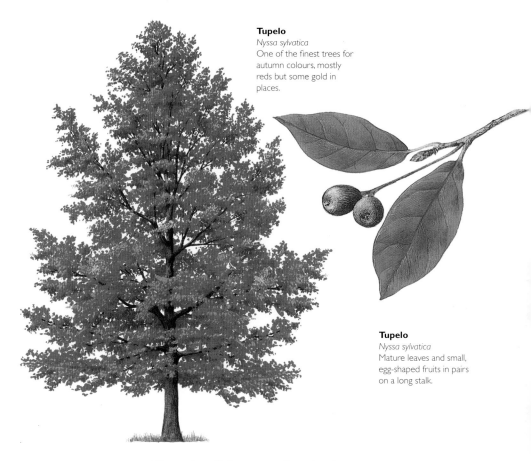

Tupelo
Nyssa sylvatica
One of the finest trees for autumn colours, mostly reds but some gold in places.

Tupelo
Nyssa sylvatica
Mature leaves and small, egg-shaped fruits in pairs on a long stalk.

Tupelo *(Nyssa sylvatica)*

Tupelos are closely related to the dogwoods (*Cornus*) and dove trees (*Davidia involucrata*). The American tupelo (*Nyssa sylvatica*) is the most common species.

Tupelo or black gum *(Nyssa sylvatica)*
Native only to eastern North America but planted in many other temperate countries for its superb show of red and gold autumn colours. In America it reaches 30m (100ft) tall but elsewhere it is seldom above 15–20m (50–70ft), with a broadly conic crown, flattening out with age, and many level branches often turning up at the ends. The red-brown buds are small and pointed, the glossy green leaves variable in both size and shape, from 5–12cm (2–5in) long, usually entire but sometimes with a few coarse teeth, normally oval and broadly pointed on a short stalk, occasionally longer and more elliptic. Both male and female flowers are inconspicuous, the former tiny yellow-green beads up to 4mm (⅛in) in diameter, the latter cylindric, about 4mm (⅛in) long, and green with purple tips. The fruit, a blue-black, egg-shaped berry, 1.5cm (½in) long, usually sets in pairs. Tupelo bark is grey and coarsely fissured into irregular rough narrow plates.

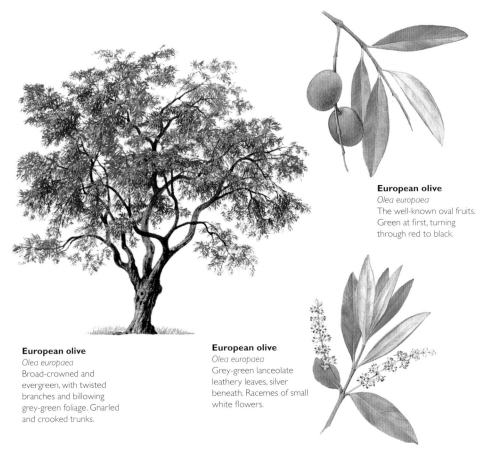

European olive
Olea europaea
The well-known oval fruits.
Green at first, turning
through red to black.

European olive
Olea europaea
Broad-crowned and
evergreen, with twisted
branches and billowing
grey-green foliage. Gnarled
and crooked trunks.

European olive
Olea europaea
Grey-green lanceolate
leathery leaves, silver
beneath. Racemes of small
white flowers.

European Olive *(Olea europaea)*

The olives belong to the large family Oleaceae. Spread right across the world, there are about 20 trees represented in the true *Olea* group, by far the most important of which is the European olive (*Olea europaea*).

European olive *(Olea europaea)*

This is native to Asia Minor and Syria. It has been cultivated since prehistoric times and is now grown all over the Mediterranean region.

The lanceolate, or narrowly ovoid, opposite evergreen leaves, 5–8cm (2–3in) long, grey-green above, silvery beneath, are leathery and pitted; the small white flowers, 0.5cm (¼in), are in racemes, 3–6cm (1¼–2½in) long; the familiar oval fruits, about 2–3cm (¾–1¼in) long, containing one hard stone, are green at first but slowly turn through red to black.

Olive trees grow slowly, reaching a maximum height of about 15m (50ft), and are nearly always pruned to keep the branches low for harvesting. Old trees have a rugged, gnarled trunk, full of fissures, and branches twisting and curving in all directions. They live to a very great age: a number of them are between 1,000 and 1,500 years old.

Norway spruce
Picea abies
An important timber tree
with reddish brown bark.

Spruces *(Picea)*

This large group of around 50 species, including many very beautiful trees, given time, may help to break down the widespread prejudice against all conifers.

The broad characteristic of spruces are: single, needle-like leaves arranged spirally on the shoots, the lower ones often twisted at the base so that most of them are on the upper half of the twig; the needles are borne on little woody pegs, which persist after the old needles fall, making the twigs very rough, and if a fresh needle is pulled off, the twig part of the peg tears away, leaving a little white splinter attached to the base of the needle.

These features help to separate the spruces from the silver firs (*Abies*, see *pp.10–17*). The female flowers, upright at first, bend over later so that most spruce cones are pendulous and fall off the tree in one piece – unlike the upright cones of cedars (*Cedrus*) and silver firs (*Abies*), which break up while they are still present on the branches.

Spruces have a very wide distribution in the northern hemisphere, coming from Europe, Siberia, Caucasus, China, Japan, the Himalayas, Canada and America.

A selection of the main spruce species will now be considered individually.

Norway spruce
Picea abies
Fine, long, flat-scaled
cones and needles green
on all sides.

Sargent spruce
Picea brachytyla
Striking flat green needles,
pure silver beneath.
Purple-brown cones with
slightly reflexed scale-tips.

Norway spruce
(Picea abies syn. *P. excelsa)*
An important timber tree, native to Europe from the Pyrenees and the Alps to Scandinavia, and from the Balkans to Russia. It can reach 60m (200ft).

Norway spruce is the traditional species for Christmas trees and is widely planted for that purpose. The needles are shining green on both sides; the young shoots orange-brown, and the female flowers bright red; the cones are 11–17cm (4½–7in), with flattish, stiff scales. The bark is coppery brown.

There is a strange type, called 'snake spruce', which has hardly any side branches and has straggling thin shoots with the needles all round the twigs.

Sargent spruce *(Picea brachytyla)*
Unfortunately this beautiful Chinese tree has been ruthlessly cut for timber and is now much less common, but it is a fine ornamental species, with silver-backed needles and purple-brown cones.

Brewer's spruce *(Picea brewerana)*
From the mountains of northwest California and southwest Oregon, this is one of the most beautiful of all conifers for ornamental planting. It is seldom above 35m (120ft), but with wonderful curtains

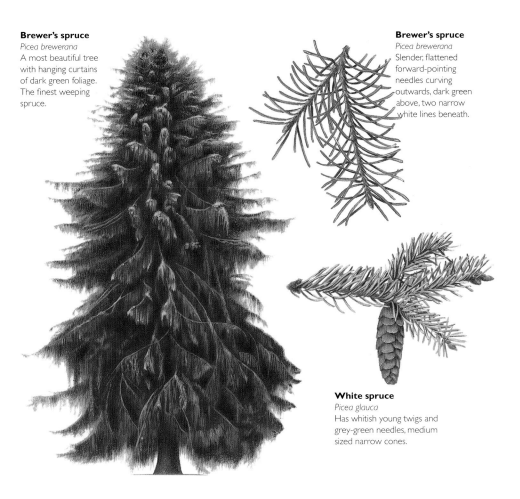

Brewer's spruce
Picea brewerana
A most beautiful tree
with hanging curtains
of dark green foliage.
The finest weeping
spruce.

Brewer's spruce
Picea brewerana
Slender, flattened
forward-pointing
needles curving
outwards, dark green
above, two narrow
white lines beneath.

White spruce
Picea glauca
Has whitish young twigs and
grey-green needles, medium
sized narrow cones.

of dark drooping side shoots hanging from each downward-sweeping branch, with hardly any lateral growth between the branches, giving a unique and very beautiful form.

The flat, dark green, shining needles, 2–3.5cm (¾–1½in) long, point forwards and curve outwards with two thin silver lines on the underside. The cones are smaller, 8–12cm (3–5in), the female flowers dark red.

Engelmann spruce *(Picea engelmannii)*
This is a mountain tree of northwestern America and Canada, about the same size as white spruce *(Picea glauca)*. The blue-green needles are 2–3cm (¾–1¼in) long, soft and flexible, but with sharp points and a foetid smell when bruised; the cones, 4–9cm (1½–3½in) long, with thin scales and toothed margins, are shining brown when ripe, the bark reddish brown, resinous and scaly.

There is an attractive bluer cultivar, 'Glauca', for ornamental planting.

White spruce *(Picea glauca* syn. *P. alba)*
Native from Alaska to Newfoundland, this is one of the most widespread conifers in Canada. Growing up to 55m (180ft) along the Peace River, but more usually to about 35m (120ft), white spruce is of

Serbian spruce
Picea omorika
A tree of most lovely form, narrow and spire-like with lower branches bending down and sweeping up again. An excellent ornamental species.

Black spruce
Picea mariana
Small, short, fat cones. Slender, soft needles crowded densely with those on top pointing forwards.

Serbian spruce
Picea omorika
Flat, broad, dark green needles, many forward-pointing, with two white bands beneath.

narrow form with almost white young shoots. The short, stiff, slender needles, about 1.5cm (½in) long, have a pungent smell when crushed and are almost round in section, with a bluish tinge due to fine white lines on all surfaces. The cones are small, tapering cylinders, 5–6cm (2–2½in) long, brown when ripe.

Koyama's spruce *(Picea koyamai)*
A Japanese species, valued for its conic shape, ascending branches and beautiful cones, 5–10cm (2–4in) long, usually very colourful, at first green-edged purple, then lilac-brown and finally pinkish brown with silvery edges to the scales.

Likiang spruce *(Picea likiangensis)*
This fine tree, up to 35m (120ft) tall and 3m (10ft) girth from southwest China, is ornamental, noted for its masses of flowers. The males are red at first, opening to golden cylinders, while the females are erect, scarlet and about 2cm (¾in) high.

Black spruce
(Picea mariana syn. P. nigra)
With the same amazingly wide native distribution as white spruce *(Picea glauca)*, this species is smaller, maximum about 30m (100ft). It differs from white spruce in having white lines only on the underside of the needles, the upper surface

Oriental spruce
Picea orientalis
Broadly conic with densely foliaged, rather crooked branches. A rather dark tree.

Oriental spruce
Picea orientalis
Very short, shiny, dark green, square-section needles. Small cones.

being dark green. The twigs are pinkish brown and slightly hairy; the cones, usually crowded in large numbers on the branches, are shorter, 3–4cm (1¼–1½in) in length.

Serbian spruce *(Picea omorika)*
A tree of quite different shape, the Serbian spruce has a very slender, spire-like form, with short upper branches ascending or horizontal, while the lower ones droop but turn up at the ends, resulting in a very beautiful tree that is rightly finding its way into more parks and gardens. Its flat, dark green needles have two broad silver bands beneath, and the

female flowers, 1.5–2.5cm (½–1in) high, are crimson. The cones, 4–6cm (1½–2½in) long, are pointed, very resinous, a remarkable blackish blue for a while, turning dark brown when ripe, and are very numerous towards the top of the tree.

Oriental spruce *(Picea orientalis)*
This large tree, up to 55m (180ft) tall, with a girth of up to 3m (10ft) in its native Asia Minor and Caucasus, is recognized by its very short needles, 0.5–1cm (¼–½in), the shortest of any spruce. The needles are shiny dark green, round ended and set on hairy pale

Colorado spruce
Picea pungens 'Glauca'
Narrowly conic tree of
wonderful silver-blue
colour.

Colorado spruce
Picea pungens 'Glauca'
Beautiful silver-blue
foliage with stiff,
forward-pointing
needles almost all
round the shoots.

Tiger tail spruce
Picea polita
Remarkable for its very
sharp, rigid, pointed, curved
radiating needles, the
stoutest of any spruce.

brown shoots. The cones, 5–8cm (2–3in) long, are curved, pointed, resinous and grey-brown when ripe.

Tiger tail spruce *(Picea polita)*

The fascination of this ornamental Japanese tree lies in its sickle-shaped needles, which are 1.5–2cm (½–¾in) long, stout, rigid, set all round its shoots, and with very sharp, hard points. It is of narrow conic form, slow growing, and with large cones, up to 10 x 4.5cm (4 x 1¾in) when open.

Colorado or blue spruce

(Picea pungens)

Native to Colorado, eastern Utah and New Mexico, this high elevation tree ranges in habitat from 1,800–3,000m (5,904–9,840ft). It has attractive bluish, stiff needles.

The Colorado spruce has given rise to many beautiful cultivars selected from the bluest wild forms. These go under the general name of *Picea pungens* 'Glauca', but are further identified by cultivar names such as: 'Koster', 'Moerheimii', 'Thomsen', and 'Spekii', and include many very striking trees with colours ranging from very blue to almost silver; these trees are much in demand for parks and gardens.

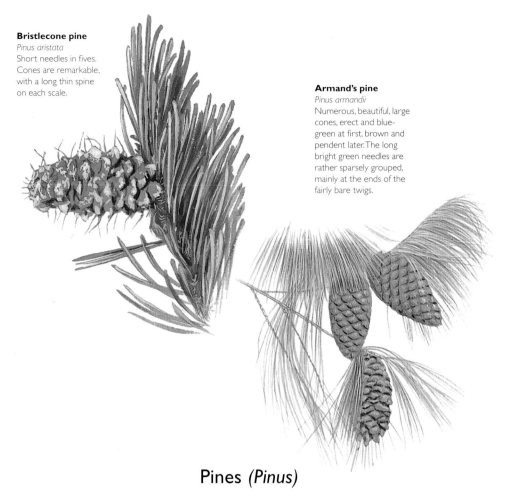

Bristlecone pine
Pinus aristata
Short needles in fives.
Cones are remarkable,
with a long thin spine
on each scale.

Armand's pine
Pinus armandii
Numerous, beautiful, large
cones, erect and blue-
green at first, brown and
pendent later. The long
bright green needles are
rather sparsely grouped,
mainly at the ends of the
fairly bare twigs.

Pines *(Pinus)*

Pines have a vast range, from the Arctic Circle to the equator. Some possess extraordinary rugged hardiness, while others need warm conditions to grow well. They are one of the world's greatest sources of timber, and are also highly ornamental.

The outstanding general characteristic of pines is that their evergreen leaves are in the form of long narrow 'needles', in bunches of twos, threes or fives. The number of needles in a bunch is almost constant for each species, which helps with their identification.

Most of the buds are brownish or red-dish brown, many are pointed though some are more cylindrical with rounded tips; they are often very resinous.

The male flowers are usually small and ovoid, in dense clusters at the base of new shoots, often orange or pinkish before opening to shed their clouds of golden pollen; the female flowers are tiny red globes at the tips of the newly expanding shoots. Most mature pines have rough, often deeply fissured bark scaling off in irregular plates.

Pine cones vary enormously in size and shape from small and almost round to very long and thin, and are formed of

Mexican white pine
Pinus ayacahuite
Young trees have a fairly
open form, becoming
denser with age. The
lower branches grow
long and level.

overlapping scales, each concealing a pair of seeds, usually winged. The cones vary in weight from a few grams to 2kg (4½lb).

In form most young pines are conic, with narrowly pointed tops, but later usually become broader and more rounded at the top.

Bristlecone pine
(Pinus aristata syn. Pinus longaeva)
With a very limited distribution in the arid mountain regions of California, Nevada, Utah and Colorado, this species is of unique interest because certain specimens (recently dubbed *Pinus longaeva*) are the oldest living things on earth. Its special fea-

ture, apart from longevity, is its small spine-covered cones, 4–7cm (1½–3in) long and often very resinous. The dense short needles, 4–7cm (1½–3in) long, are in fives; its new shoots carry orange-coloured pubescence and the trunks of old specimens are twisted and very large.

Armand's pine *(Pinus armandii)*
Native to the mountains of west China, this is planted mainly for its beautiful cones, up to 18 x 9cm (7 x 3½in), erect in the first year, pendulous the next year, blue-green at first then changing to light brown with red-brown inside the scales, which are thick, large and often resinous.

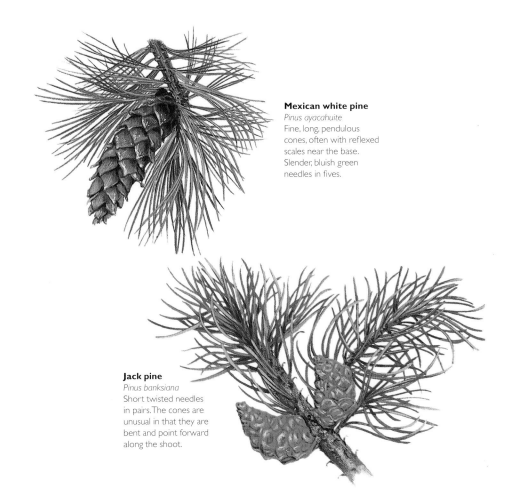

Mexican white pine
Pinus ayacahuite
Fine, long, pendulous cones, often with reflexed scales near the base. Slender, bluish green needles in fives.

Jack pine
Pinus banksiana
Short twisted needles in pairs. The cones are unusual in that they are bent and point forward along the shoot.

The needles are in fives, 12–14cm (5–5½in) long, with a drooping habit.

Knobcone pine *(Pinus attenuata)*

Native to southwestern USA, this tree is of special interest because of its amazing asymmetrical cones, 10–14cm (4–5½in) long, with stout spines on the scales and remaining on the branches in bunches for many years.

Mexican white pine *(Pinus ayacahuite)*

This tree has a natural range from Mexico to Guatemala and is planted for its beauty in many countries. Its special features are fine pendulous cones, 20–40cm (8–16in) long x 6–12cm (2½–5in) broad when open, having stout 2cm (¾in) stalks and usually markedly reflexed scales, especially near the base; the long level branches are clothed in slender needles, 12–15cm (5–6in) long, in bundles of five. The tree grows up to a height of 50m (160ft).

Jack pine *(Pinus banksiana)*

Native to Canada from near the Arctic Circle to the Great Lakes, this small, two-needled pine is one of the hardiest of all trees, tolerating severe conditions of exposure, low temperatures, poor soils and low rainfall. Its special characteristic is its cones, which are 3–6cm (1¼–2½in)

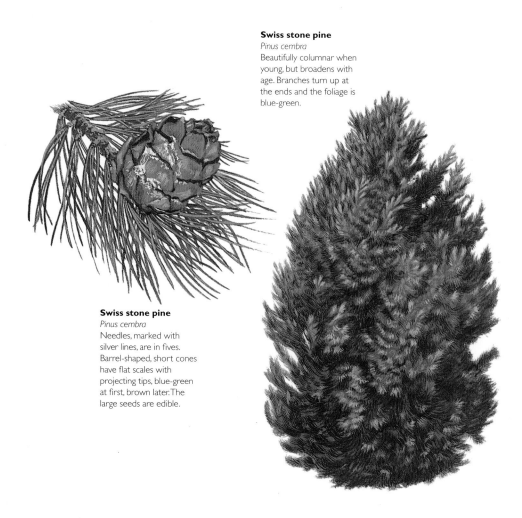

Swiss stone pine
Pinus cembra
Beautifully columnar when young, but broadens with age. Branches turn up at the ends and the foliage is blue-green.

Swiss stone pine
Pinus cembra
Needles, marked with silver lines, are in fives. Barrel-shaped, short cones have flat scales with projecting tips, blue-green at first, brown later. The large seeds are edible.

long, ovoid, pointed and bent so that they face forward along the shoot.

Lace bark pine *(Pinus bungeana)*

This tree is native to China, and is remarkable for its beautiful bark which flakes away, as in a plane tree (*Platanus*), resulting in chalky white irregular patches scattered in a grey-green matrix. The cones are very attractive, barrel-shaped, up to 5 x 4cm (2 x 1½in), with a small number of large scales with sharp spines. The pine needles, 6–8cm (2½–3in) long, are arranged in threes.

Swiss stone pine or Arolla
(Pinus cembra)

This beautiful pine, native to the Alps, the Carpathians and Siberia, is a perfect part of the wild mountain scenery. Its seeds yield one of the edible 'pine kernels' collected in quantity, especially in Russia. Both the foliage and the cones are very attractive; the needles are in fives, 7–9cm (3–3½in) long, and marked with blue-white lines, while the barrel-shaped cones, about 8 x 6cm (3 x 2½in), are at first blue-green but later brown and have

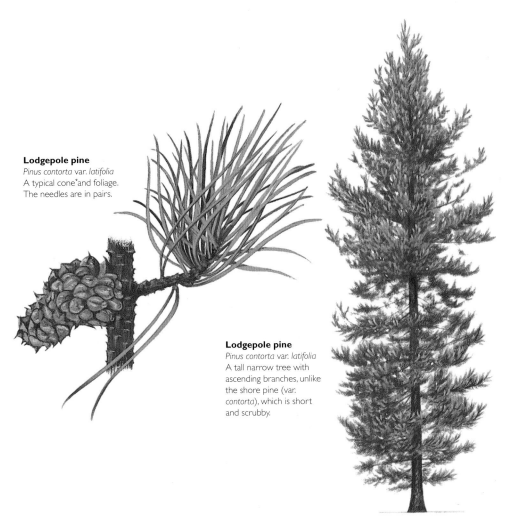

Lodgepole pine
Pinus contorta var. *latifolia*
A typical cone and foliage.
The needles are in pairs.

Lodgepole pine
Pinus contorta var. *latifolia*
A tall narrow tree with
ascending branches, unlike
the shore pine (var.
contorta), which is short
and scrubby.

two large edible seeds behind each scale.

Shore pine and Lodgepole pine
(Pinus contorta)

The species *Pinus contorta* is usually divided into two separate varieties — beach or shore pine (*Pinus contorta* var. *contorta*) and lodgepole pine (*P. contorta* var. *latifolia*).

The shore pine ranges from southeastern Alaska to California, a short scrubby tree, but useful because it is tolerant of sea-winds and bad soils. The paired needles are short (4–5cm/1½–2in) and twisted (hence the name *contorta*) and the cones are about 5cm (2in) long, pointing down the stem, with prickles on the scales.

The lodgepole pine, so called because it was used for the support poles for the huts of North American Indians, grows further inland, from the Yukon to Colorado, with a great range of elevation, 450–3,200m (1,476–10,496ft). It is taller and straighter than the shore pine.

The needles of the lodgepole pine are slightly longer than those of the shore pine and are not as densely set.

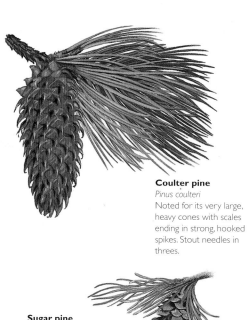

Coulter pine
Pinus coulteri
Noted for its very large, heavy cones with scales ending in strong, hooked spikes. Stout needles in threes.

Sugar pine
Pinus lambertiana
Stiff, twisted needles in fives. Cones up to 50cm (20in) long, the longest of all pines.

Sugar pine
Pinus lambertiana
A fine tree of stately form but subject to blister rust.

Coulter pine or big cone pine
(Pinus coulteri)

This southwest Californian tree is famous for its huge oblong-ovoid cones, up to 35cm (14in) long x 20cm (8in) broad, and weighing anything up to 2kg (4lb), with thick scales each mounted with a strong hooked spike like an eagle's claw. The tree grows to about 30m (100ft) tall, has a fairly broad crown and very rugged bark. Its needles are in threes, rather glaucous, stiff, stout and 20–28cm (8–11in) long.

Slash pine *(Pinus elliottii)*

A native range from the coastal plain of South Carolina to central Florida and Louisiana. A rapid grower, making 1.5m (5ft) annual shoots on good sites and usually reaching about 30m (100ft) in height. The needles, 20–30cm (8–12in) long, vary in numbers in a bunch from two to five. The young shoots are glaucous and the cones, 9–13cm (3½–5in) long, are on short stalks.

Sugar pine *(Pinus lambertiana)*

This tree gets its name from a sugary exudation obtained from the heartwood, which has sometimes been used as a sugar substitute. A native of Oregon and California and the most valuable of all the

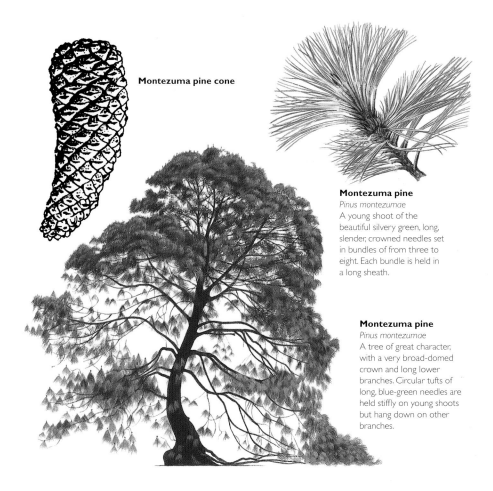

Montezuma pine cone

Montezuma pine
Pinus montezumae
A young shoot of the beautiful silvery green, long, slender, crowned needles set in bundles of from three to eight. Each bundle is held in a long sheath.

Montezuma pine
Pinus montezumae
A tree of great character, with a very broad-domed crown and long lower branches. Circular tufts of long, blue-green needles are held stiffly on young shoots but hang down on other branches.

pines, growing up to 75m (250ft) in height and to a diameter of 3m (10ft). It is a tree of magnificent form, with a long clean trunk and a fine crown clothed in stiff, twisted needles, 8–11cm (3–4½in) long, and in bundles of five. It has the longest of all pine cones, 30–50cm (12–20in), on stalks 7–10cm (3–4in).

Montezuma pine *(Pinus montezumae)*
A decidedly tender Mexican pine that will not stand hard winters, this is one of the most unusual and beautiful trees, with its wide spreading rounded crown, marvellous blue-grey needles, 25–40cm (10–16in) long, slender and spreading stiffly round the shoots. The small cones, 6–10cm (2½–4in) long, are barrel shaped and with small prickles on the scales.

Bishop pine *(Pinus muricata)*
Native along the California coast, the strong point about this tree is its remarkable resistance to salty winds, and in many countries it is an obvious choice for coastal shelter belts.

This is often called prickly pine because of its special botanical feature — obliquely ovoid, prickly cones, about 8 x 6cm (3 x 2½in), in regular whorls of from three to seven, that still remain on the branches for anything up to 40 years and

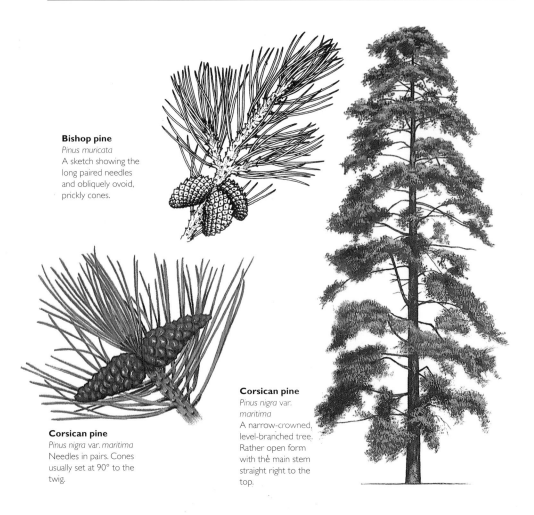

Bishop pine
Pinus muricata
A sketch showing the
long paired needles
and obliquely ovoid,
prickly cones.

Corsican pine
Pinus nigra var. *maritima*
Needles in pairs. Cones
usually set at 90° to the
twig.

Corsican pine
Pinus nigra var.
maritima
A narrow-crowned,
level-branched tree.
Rather open form
with the main stem
straight right to the
top.

are often found still on trunks up to
50cm (20in) in diameter. The paired needles are 7–15cm (3–6in) long, the cylindrical buds often coated with white resin.

Austrian pine
(Pinus nigra var. austriaca)

Native to Austria, central Italy and the
Balkans, this is another species emi-
nently suitable for shelter belts, even
close to the coast, but it has the unusual
advantage of tolerating alkaline and clay
soils. The dense, paired, stiff needles,
8–14cm (3–5½in) long, are very dark
green and unusually resistant to smoke
and fumes. The cones are pointed,
narrow ovoid, 5–8cm (2–3in) long, set at
a wide angle to the stems.

Corsican pine
(Pinus nigra var. maritima)

Not as hardy as its close relation, Austrian pine (*Pinus nigra* var. *austriaca*),
Corsican pine is a larger, faster growing,
more finely branched tree native to Corsica, southern Italy and Sicily. Growing
best on light soils, with fairly low rainfall,
it grows to about 45m (150ft) high and
1.5m (5ft) in diameter, and its paired
needles, 12–18cm (5–7in) long, are not
as stiff as those of Austrian pine. The
buds are pointed and often coated with

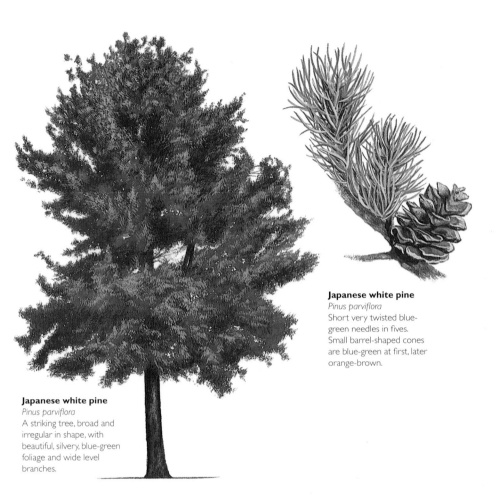

Japanese white pine
Pinus parviflora
Short very twisted blue-green needles in fives. Small barrel-shaped cones are blue-green at first, later orange-brown.

Japanese white pine
Pinus parviflora
A striking tree, broad and irregular in shape, with beautiful, silvery, blue-green foliage and wide level branches.

white resin, and the cones are the same as for Austrian pine, approximately 5–8cm (2–3in) long.

Longleaf pine (*Pinus palustris*)

Longleaf pine is not a large tree, the tallest being 32m (105ft) with a diameter of just over 1m (3ft). It prefers a warm humid climate and is native to the south-eastern corner of the USA. It has the longest needles of all the pines — up to 45cm (18in), and arranged in threes; they are slender and flexible.

The pine cones are large, 15–25cm (6–10in) long x 5–8cm (2–3in) broad, nut brown when ripe.

Japanese white pine (*Pinus parviflora*)

Specially pruned specimens and dwarf forms of this tree are a common feature in the design of many Japanese parks and gardens, and it is also one of the main trees used in Bonsai dwarfing for indoor use. The larger forms of this species grow up to 17m (56ft) tall. The form of this pine is unusual, with wide level or drooping branches and short needles, 4–8cm (1½–3in), somewhat twisted and of a beautiful blue-green colour. The cones are barrel shaped when open, up to 6 x 4cm (2½ x 1½in), and when ripe they are rich shades of brown.

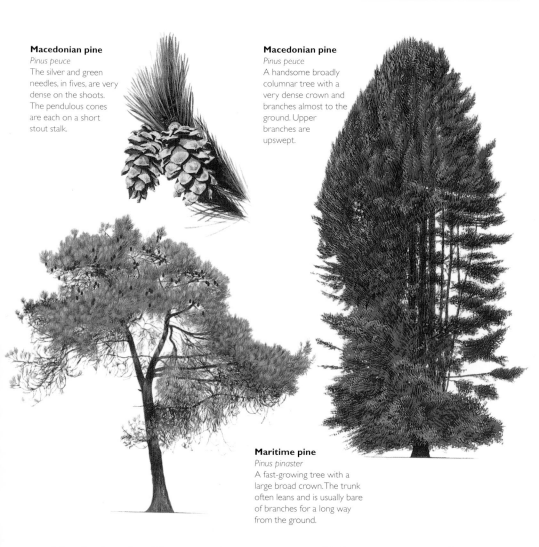

Macedonian pine
Pinus peuce
The silver and green needles, in fives, are very dense on the shoots. The pendulous cones are each on a short stout stalk.

Macedonian pine
Pinus peuce
A handsome broadly columnar tree with a very dense crown and branches almost to the ground. Upper branches are upswept.

Maritime pine
Pinus pinaster
A fast-growing tree with a large broad crown. The trunk often leans and is usually bare of branches for a long way from the ground.

Macedonian pine *(Pinus peuce)*
This is a very attractive pine for ornamental planting and is not fussy about soil conditions. Native to the southwest Balkans, it grows to 30m (100ft) tall in a fairly broad columnar form and has beautiful silver stomata lines on its densely set needles, 8–12cm (3–5in) long, curved at the base, resinous, green at first then ripening to a rich brown.

Maritime pine *(Pinus pinaster)*
This rather coarse, rapidly growing, two-needled pine, native to the central and west Mediterranean region, does not succeed in cold climates or on heavy soils but is used on a large scale in the light sandy areas of southwest France. One of its special features is its large cones, 12–18cm (5–7in) long, in whorls of three to six, green at first, then a wonderful chocolate colour and finally a rich shining brown, eventually shedding seeds with large shining wings.

Stone pine *(Pinus pinea)*
With its large umbrella-shaped crown, stone pine is the most distinctive tree,

Maritime pine
Pinus pinaster
Long stout needles in
pairs. Cones large, bright
brown when ripe, and in
bunches of two to seven.

Stone pine
Pinus pinea
A large and beautiful cone
with thick, hard scales,
much larger on one side
than on the other. Stout
needles in pairs.

Stone pine
Pinus pinea
This unique umbrella-
shaped, wide crown is a
well-known feature of the
Mediterranean region. The
heavy, low branches are
often almost level.

together with the Italian cypress
(*Cupressus sempervirens*), along the
Mediterranean from Portugal to Asia
Minor. Apart from its shape, its distinctive
features are its large, hard, ovoid or nearly
round brown cones, 10–13cm (4–5in) long
x 8–10cm (3–4in) broad, with thick
rounded scales which hide the very best
and largest edible pine kernels, which are
very much in demand.

The stout needles, 12–15cm (5–6in)
long, are in pairs and the dark bark is fissured with reddish markings.

Ponderosa pine (*Pinus ponderosa*)
The most widely distributed of all the
native North American pines, with huge
areas in the northwest and found at elevations from sea level to 3,000m
(9,840ft), this is one of the largest and
most important timber trees in the USA,
growing up to 70m (230ft) high and 2.5m
(8ft) in diameter and living to a great age
— sometimes to over 700 years.

With its very deep tap-root it can grow
where many species fail. Botanical features include needles in threes, 16–22cm

Ponderosa pine
Pinus ponderosa
Mature cones and long
dark needles in threes.

Ponderosa pine
Pinus ponderosa
Conic in form with rather
open crown and dark
green foliage. Straight
trunk and orange-brown
bark.

Monterey pine
Pinus radiata
Bright green, slender
needles in threes. Cones
large and asymmetrical, in
bunches of three to five.

(6–9in) long, and crowded on the shoots; cones 7–10cm (3–4in) long, leaving the base on the branches when they are shed, and attractive orange and brown bark, with scaly irregular plates. *Pinus jeffreyi* is very close to *ponderosa* but has larger cones, 15–18cm (6–7in) long.

Monterey pine *(Pinus radiata)*
Only native to one or two very small areas on the Monterey peninsula and in Cambria, California, this remarkable pine has quickly become of importance owing to its extraordinarily rapid growth and large size; it is now used in the forests of America, Europe, South Africa, Australia and New Zealand, becoming a major species in the last two countries. It grows to over 60m (200ft) with diameters up to 2m (6ft), and in mild winters continues to grow throughout the year. Annual shoots of 2m (6ft) are common (one Australian tree is on record for growing 6m/ 20ft) in its fifth year). The needles are in threes, bright green, slender and dense, 10–15cm (4–6in). The pine cones are up to 15 x 9cm (6 x 3½in)

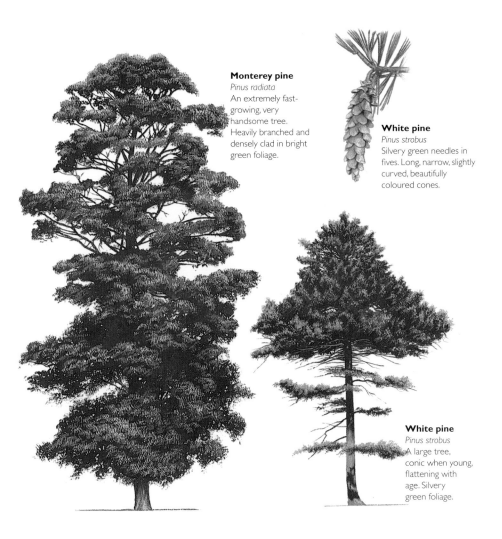

Monterey pine
Pinus radiata
An extremely fast-growing, very handsome tree. Heavily branched and densely clad in bright green foliage.

White pine
Pinus strobus
Silvery green needles in fives. Long, narrow, slightly curved, beautifully coloured cones.

White pine
Pinus strobus
A large tree, conic when young, flattening with age. Silvery green foliage.

and very asymmetrical at the base, in whorls of three to six and retained on both branches and trunks for many years, in a similar way to those of bishop pine (*Pinus muricata*). The bark is very rugged, with deep fissures.

Northern pitch pine *(Pinus rigida)*
The needles are in threes, 8–12cm (3–5in) long, and the cones small, 3–6cm (1¼–2½in).

Digger pine *(Pinus sabiniana)*
A Californian tree with large cones — reaching up to 24cm (10in) long and 16cm (6in) wide when open, and with short hooks on its scales. It has distinctive grey-green foliage.

White or Weymouth pine
(Pinus strobus)
This tree of eastern North America is a large tree, reaching 65m (210ft) tall with a diameter of 3m (10ft). The silvery-green needles are in fives, 8–12cm (3–5in) and the slightly curved, narrow cones, 10–20cm (4–8in) long, with rather broad thin scales, are often resinous and hang down on slender stalks.

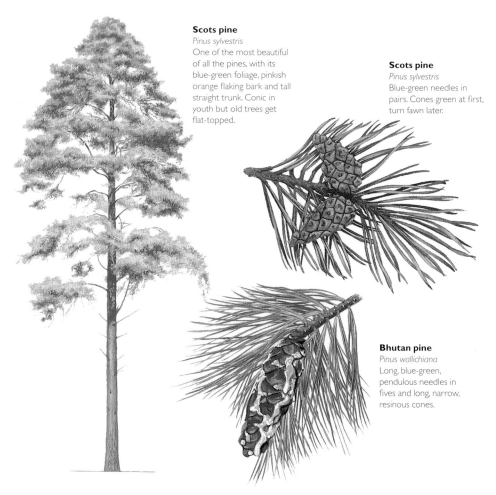

Scots pine
Pinus sylvestris
One of the most beautiful of all the pines, with its blue-green foliage, pinkish orange flaking bark and tall straight trunk. Conic in youth but old trees get flat-topped.

Scots pine
Pinus sylvestris
Blue-green needles in pairs. Cones green at first, turn fawn later.

Bhutan pine
Pinus wallichiana
Long, blue-green, pendulous needles in fives and long, narrow, resinous cones.

Scots pine *(Pinus sylvestris)*

This has a wide range from Scotland to Siberia and Lapland to Spain. Its special features are its beautiful blue-green paired needles, 5–10cm (2–4in) long, and the unique pinkish orange flaking bark in the upper parts of the tree. Its pointed ovoid cones are 5–8cm (2–3in) long, green at first, becoming light brown as they mature and round when fully open.

Japanese black pine *(Pinus thunbergii)*

Another Japanese pine much used for Bonsai dwarfing, but in natural forests this grows much larger than the Japanese white pine *(Pinus parviflora)*, up to 40m (130ft) with diameters up to 2m (6ft). The small cones, 3–6cm (1¼–2½in) long, are usually in large bunches, sometimes of as many as 40 or 50. The needles are in pairs, 7–10cm (3–4in) long, pointing forwards and dense on the shoots.

Bhutan pine *(Pinus wallichiana)*

Found growing in the wild from Afghanistan to Nepal at high elevations, 1,800–3,700m (5,904–12,136ft), this is a very ornamental tree. Its distinctive features include long, lax, blue-green needles in fives, 16–22cm (6–9in), and beautiful narrow resinous cones, 20–30cm (8–12in) long.

124

London plane
Platanus × hispanica
Typical leaves and seed balls.

London plane
Platanus × hispanica
Very large tree, shown here in summer and winter, which succeeds well in towns. Bark flakes off leaving creamy patches. Seed balls remain over winter.

Planes *(Platanus)*

The trees described here belong to the Platanaceae family and are known in England as planes. Confusion occurs because Americans call them sycamores.

London plane

(Platanus × hispanica syn.
P. × acerifolia)

This magnificent tree, often exceeding 35m (120ft) in height, is ideal for town planting in parks, squares and boulevards and is a famous feature of London. It is wind-firm, resistant to smoke and fumes and, if space is restricted, it will stand repeated and severe cutting back with no ill effects. It is a fast grower,

often putting on 1–2m (3–6ft) a year when young, and in open ground develops a majestic crown of large, spreading, twisting branches, beautiful in winter, and, in summer, clothed with striking, large, five-lobed, maple-like leaves, up to 20 x 23cm (8 x 9in) arranged alternately.

Other special characteristics are bark that flakes off in irregular patches to give a lovely mottled pattern; seeds in hanging balls up to 4cm (1½in) across; and leaf stalks whose bases encircle and enclose the next year's buds, which when mature are red-brown, ovoid and with slightly curved tips.

Buttonwood
Platanus occidentalis
Shallow-lobed leaves. Seed
balls are less spiny than in
oriental plane.

Oriental plane
Platanus orientalis
Typical deeply cut leaves
and seed balls.

Buttonwood or American sycamore
(Platanus occidentalis)

This is the largest broadleaved tree in
America, with heights up to 53m (170ft)
and girth up to 16m (52ft); it ranges
across all the states east of the Great
Plains except for Minnesota.

Of very rapid early growth, it has a
narrower crown and straighter trunk
than the oriental plane (*Platanus orientalis*). Buttonwood leaves normally have
only three distinct lobes, which are shallowly divided; the seed balls are
smoother than those of other planes and
usually only have one ball to each stalk.

Oriental plane or chinar
(Platanus orientalis)

Native to southeast Europe, Asia Minor
and Kashmir, this is even larger and
more vigorous than the London plane
(*Platanus × hispanica*), but less hardy
and less common. The oriental plane is
one of the longest-living broadleaved
trees, often exceeding 500 years. Many
exceed 45m (150ft), with a girth over
15m (50ft); they have deeply cut, five-
lobed leaves, up to 18 x 20cm (7 x 8in),
and a very broad crown, with a crooked
trunk and large limbs. The fruit balls are
smaller than those of the London plane.

White poplar
Populus alba
Crown shows silver as
leaves turn in the wind.
Shown here in summer
and winter.

Poplars *(Populus)*

Poplars are famous for their rapid growth, long-stalked trembling leaves and large colourful catkins. Over 30 species of this genus grow in northern temperate regions. There are four main groups, with similar characteristics:

• White poplars: the leaves are white below, and on top when just opened; the new shoots are also white. The catkins are crimson and grey and the bark is pitted with small diamond-shaped boles.

• Balsam poplars: the winter buds and young leaves are aromatic, the bud scales are sticky, the leaves are large and the catkins are long and attractive.

• Black poplars and their hybrids: a large group, including many hybrids and special clones; only a few characteristics apply to them all. Their leaves, none of which have white undersides, appear comparatively late in the season and have compressed slender stalks. Most old trees have rugged bark.

• Aspens: trees in this group have roundish leaves with long lateral stalks, which are in constant movement. They sucker freely and are not easy to raise from cuttings.

White poplar *(Populus alba)*
This white poplar is a European tree,

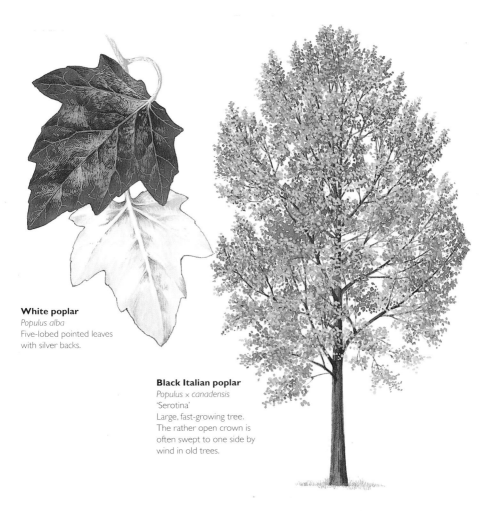

White poplar
Populus alba
Five-lobed pointed leaves
with silver backs.

Black Italian poplar
Populus x canadensis
'Serotina'
Large, fast-growing tree.
The rather open crown is
often swept to one side by
wind in old trees.

rarely taller than 25m (80ft); the trunk is seldom upright and the branches twist; the twigs are very white when young. It is canker-resistant. The three- to five-lobed leaves are 4–6cm (1½–2½in) across, with brilliant silver undersides, making a beautiful picture when blown by the wind and seen against a blue sky.

Balsam poplar or 'Tacamahaca'
(Populus balsamifera)
This American balsam poplar is smaller than the black cottonwood (*Populus tri chocarpa*), and sends up many suckers. The vigorous 'TT20' is a cross between this and *P. trichocarpa*.

Black Italian poplar
(Populus x canadensis 'Serotina')
Widespread throughout Europe, this very large black poplar, up to 42m (140ft), originally a French hybrid, has large branches, fairly level at first, then sweeping upwards to form an open wide crown, often one-sided. It has long red catkins, up to 12cm (5in).

There is a cultivar with golden leaves, 'Serotina Aurea'.

Balm of Gilead or Ontario poplar
(Populus x candicans)
This is a highly scented species but it is particularly susceptible to canker and

Black Italian poplar
Populus × canadensis 'Serotina'
Leaves truncate at base on long, flattened, often pink stalks.

Balm of Gilead poplar
Populus × candicans 'Aurora'
Variegated cultivar. Leaves are a patchwork of white, green and cream, often with pink areas.

Grey poplar
Populus canescens
Leaves vary from almost round with shallow, curved irregular serrations to short pointed five-lobed form. Greyish white below and on long, flattened stalks.

suckers prolifically. It is one of the balsam poplars.

There is a cultivar 'Aurora', with cream and pink patches on the leaves.

Grey poplar (*Populus canescens*)

One of the white poplars, from Europe and western Asia. It is larger than the white poplar (*Populus alba*), but neither the twigs nor the rounded leaves are quite as white.

Chinese necklace poplar
(*Populus lasiocarpa*)

A particularly attractive Chinese tree, *Populus lasiocarpa* is outside the previously mentioned groups. It grows to 20m

(70ft) and has enormous heart-shaped leaves, up to 35cm (14in) long, with red stalks and midribs. The common name is derived from the little round green fruits strung along the ripe catkins.

True black poplar (*Populus nigra*)

This black poplar is one of the original European species but is seldom planted now and is becoming rare. It grows up to 35m (120ft) tall, with many large branches, mostly ascending, and is domed at the top when old; large burrs are usual on the short stout trunk. It has crimson catkins. It is one of the parents of many good hybrid species of poplar.

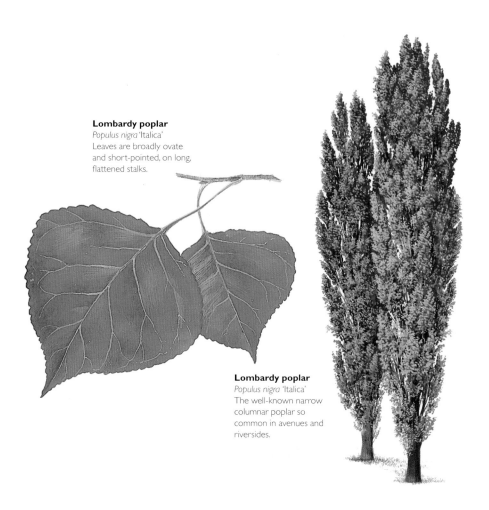

Lombardy poplar
Populus nigra 'Italica'
Leaves are broadly ovate
and short-pointed, on long,
flattened stalks.

Lombardy poplar
Populus nigra 'Italica'
The well-known narrow
columnar poplar so
common in avenues and
riversides.

Lombardy poplar
(Populus nigra 'Italica')
This well-known and much used fastigiate black poplar originated in Italy but is now common in many countries. It grows to a height of 35m (120ft), with a beautiful narrow upright form.

Aspen *(Populus tremula)*
This native tree of Europe and Asia Minor seldom grows above 20m (70ft) tall. The bark is fairly smooth with horizontal markings. The male catkins are grey and rather stout. The roundish leaves, with a few blunt teeth, are coppery at first, soon becoming grey-green.

Quaking aspen
(Populus tremuloides)
Found from Alaska to Newfoundland, and the only Californian native to reach the Arctic Circle, this aspen poplar reaches up to 30m (100ft) tall, and has finely toothed leaves and slender catkins.

Black cottonwood or western balsam
(Populus trichocarpa)
Native from Alaska to California, this scented balsam poplar is the largest American poplar, to 60m (200ft) tall. The large pointed leaves (10–30cm/4–12in) are whitish beneath; the bark tends to peel off.

Prunus 'Amanogawa'
Closely bunched pale
pink flowers.

Prunus 'Amanogawa'
The most widely used
narrowly fastigiate cherry.
Pale pink flowers.

Cherries *(Prunus)*

This is a very large group from the Rosaceae family, and is the most successful of all groups of spring-flowering trees. It includes the cherries and cherry laurels, as well as plums, apricots, peaches and almonds, and contains over 200 species from temperate regions, as well as countless hybrids and cultivars. A small representative selection will be considered here, concentrating on the wild species and the cultivated forms of special ornamental value.

Prunus 'Amanogawa'

This is an impressive fastigiate tree, which forms a very narrow column with bronze young leaves and almost upright clusters of fragrant, semi-double pale pink flowers.

American red plum
(Prunus americana)

This, the best known of the American wild plums, is native to the eastern and central states and as far south as Georgia and New Mexico. It is the ancestor of many orchard plums; a strong grower up to 10m (30ft) tall, with sharply toothed leaves, 7–11cm (3–4½in) long, and pure white flowers, 2.5cm (1in) across in stalkless umbels. The almost round fruits, about 2.5cm (1in) in diameter, are

Common apricot
Prunus armeniaca
The wild apricot has given
its name to a colour, a
slightly red orange shade.

Gean cherry
Prunus avium
A fine mature tree, shown
here in summer and winter.
Young ones have very straight
branches. Leaves are red and
yellow in the autumn.

red with yellow flesh. Closely related is *Prunus mexicana*, a larger tree which has purplish red fruits.

Common apricot *(Prunus armeniaca)*
Growing up to 10m (30ft) tall, this native of north China is a rounded-form tree with broadly ovate leaves, 6–9cm (2½–3½in) long, set with rounded teeth; the white or pale pink flowers, 2.5cm (1in) across, are set singly, and the round fruits, 3–4cm (1¼–1½in) in diameter, are yellow, tinged with red. Some of its cultivars have larger fruits.

Gean or wild cherry *(Prunus avium)*
Gean is one parent of many cultivated cherries, particularly the black-fruited ones, and is native to Europe, western Asia and North Africa. It is a tree of great vigour, up to 30m (100ft) tall, conic, with open, whorled branches when young, becoming dome-crowned with age. The bark is beautiful, greyish or reddish, with prominent horizontal bands of brown lenticel scars, and peels away across the stem like birch bark.

The pointed buds are shining red-brown and the oblong, sharply toothed pointed leaves, 7–10cm (3–4in) long, set on short grooved stalks, turn yellow and red in autumn. There are masses of

Gean cherry
Prunus avium
The white flowers and
bronze young leaves open
together, and are stunning
in spring.

Purple-leafed plum
Prunus cerasifera 'Pissardii'
Large white flowers and
purple leaves.

white flowers, 2.5–3cm (1–1¼in) across, set in clusters on stalks, 3–5cm (1¼–2in) long, and the fruit, red to blackish red when ripe, is almost round, 2–2.5cm (¾–1in) in diameter.

The cultivar 'Plena' is one of the finest double white cherries, growing to about 20m (70ft) tall; it has flowers up to 4cm (1½in) across, which appear in great profusion. It seldom sets any fruits.

Myrobalan or cherry plum
(*Prunus cerasifera*)
Native from the Balkans to central Asia, this is the earliest-flowering wild plum — often a month before the blackthorn

(*Prunus spinosa*) or the bullace (*Prunus insititia*). It is much used for hedges. Its fruits are round and red.

'Pissardii' is a cultivated variety, with purplish red leaves and white or slightly pink flowers.

Sour cherry (*Prunus cerasus*)
Native to southeast Europe and southwest Asia, and one of the parents of the 'Morello' cherry, this is a small bushy species that produces sucker growth and can be a nuisance. It has small red to blackish fruits, which are very sour-tasting. The species itself is of little importance, but its cultivar 'Rhexii', with

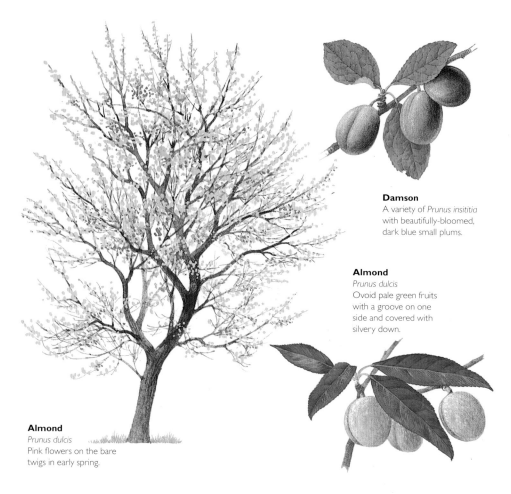

Damson
A variety of *Prunus insititia*
with beautifully-bloomed,
dark blue small plums.

Almond
Prunus dulcis
Ovoid pale green fruits
with a groove on one
side and covered with
silvery down.

Almond
Prunus dulcis
Pink flowers on the bare
twigs in early spring.

double white flowers, 3–4cm (1¼–1½in) in diameter, on long stalks, is later flowering than most cherries and is well worth growing.

Wild plum

(Prunus communis syn. P. domestica)

Probably of Asian origin, the wild plum has been naturalized in Europe for hundreds of years; it is very similar to bullace (*Prunus insititia*), but the fruits of the wild plum are always black, and oblong, not round. Crosses and varieties of both bullace and wild plum have given rise to numerous cultivated plums, including the damson.

David's peach *(Prunus davidiana)*

This Chinese tree flowers very early, so needs shelter in frost-prone areas. The twigs are grey in winter and the leaves like those of almond (*Prunus dulcis*). The pure white flowers, 2.5cm (1in) across, are produced singly; the fruits are downy, 3–4cm (1¼–1½in) in diameter, yellow, with a large pitted stone.

Almond

(Prunus dulcis syn. P. amygdalus)

This small tree, native to North Africa and western Asia, is very close to a peach and is the only common wild species. Almond is loved for its beautiful early

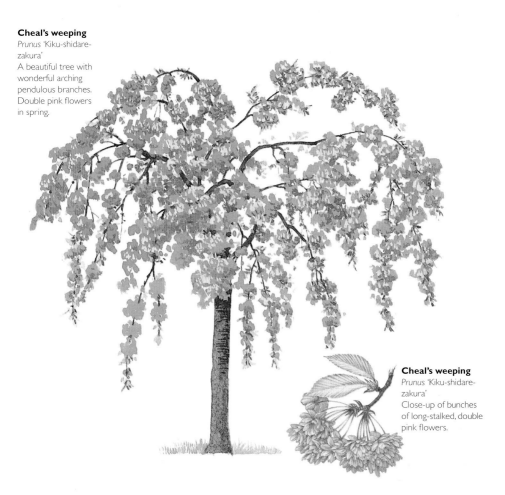

Cheal's weeping
Prunus 'Kiku-shidare-zakura'
A beautiful tree with wonderful arching pendulous branches. Double pink flowers in spring.

Cheal's weeping
Prunus 'Kiku-shidare-zakura'
Close-up of bunches of long-stalked, double pink flowers.

spring, large pink flowers, 2.5–4cm (1–1½in) across. Its leaves are finely toothed and lanceolate, 7–12cm (3–5in) long, often turning red. The light green fruits are ovoid, rather flattened, 4–5cm (1½–2in) long, grooved on one side and covered with silvery down. Inside is a pale brown pitted nut containing the well-known edible kernel.

Bullace *(Prunus insititia)*
Bullace has much the same native range as blackthorn *(Prunus spinosa)* but is much less common. The differences are as follows: bullace has larger leaves, 4–8cm (1½–3in) long, that are also more coarsely toothed; the twigs are not so thorny and have a lighter coloured bark; the flowers are larger, 1.5–2.5cm (½–1in) across; and the fruits are rounder, up to 2.5cm (1in) in diameter, and yellow or black when ripe.

Cheal's weeping
(Prunus 'Kiku-shidare-zakura')
This is a pendulous Japanese cherry, with double pink flowers in spring.

Cherry laurel *(Prunus laurocerasus)*
This very well-known species is much used for hedges and screens; native to southeast Europe and Asia Minor, it is an evergreen with large, leathery, glossy,

Cherry laurel
Prunus laurocerasus
Larger round berries.
Large leathery, glossy
leaves on yellow-green
stalks.

Cherry laurel
Prunus laurocerasus
Often grown as a hedge or
shrubbery but will form a
small tree if given space.

broadly lanceolate leaves, up to 18 x 6cm (7 x 2½in), with slightly toothed margins and stout 2cm (¾in) stalks. It grows to a maximum of 14m (46ft) and has upright spikes of small fragrant white flowers, 8–14cm (3–5½in) tall, followed by berries, 1–2cm (½–¾in) long, green at first, then red, finally turning to black. The bark is blackish brown in colour. The leaves smell of almonds if crushed, and are very poisonous.

Portugal laurel (*Prunus lusitanica*)
A strong-growing, handsome, evergreen, bushy tree from Spain and Portugal, occasionally reaching 15m (50ft) high, with oblong, ovate, leathery, coarsely toothed leaves, glossy dark green above, yellow-green on the lower surface. The buds are narrow, acute and bright red-brown. Masses of creamy white fragrant flowers grow in dense spikes, 12–23cm (5–9in) long, followed by small red berries, about 1cm (½in) long, turning black when ripe. There are several attractive cultivars of this species.

Manchurian cherry (*Prunus maackii*)
This tree from Korea and Manchuria has small, fragrant white flowers, 1cm (½in) across, in fairly round racemes. It has beautiful multicoloured bark, which has

Bird cherry
Prunus padus
Small flowers crowded on long spikes. Young leaves yellowish green at first.

Portugal laurel
Prunus lusitanica
Oval berries, turning black later. Leathery leaves on red stalks.

Wild peach
Prunus persica
A very beautiful round fruit grooved on one side, suffused with red when ripe and covered in velvety down.

mixed browns, reds, golds and greys, and peels off in horizontal strips very similar to that of birch (*Betula*).

Japanese apricot (*Prunus mume*)
This is much the same in size and form as *Prunus armeniaca* but has scented, pale rose flowers, larger, more pointed leaves, and its yellow fruits are not very palatable. It is grown for its lovely flowers. Cultivated varieties include 'Alboplena', with semi-double white flowers in winter months; 'Pendula', a weeping tree with pale pink flowers very early in the year; and 'Alphandii', which has sets of semi-double pink flowers.

Bird cherry (*Prunus padus*)
This European and Asian tree has white, fragrant flowers, densely crowded on spikes, 8–13cm (3–5in) long, some semi-upright but mostly leaning over sideways. The fruit is a small round berry, black when ripe and 6–9mm (¼–⅜in) in diameter. The slightly leathery, finely toothed leaves are 8–12cm (3–5in) long and turn yellow, with a little red, in autumn.

'Plena' has larger, double white, long-lasting flowers. 'Watereri' has long spikes, up to 20cm (8in), of single white flowers.

Wild peach (*Prunus persica*)
Although native to China, this tree has

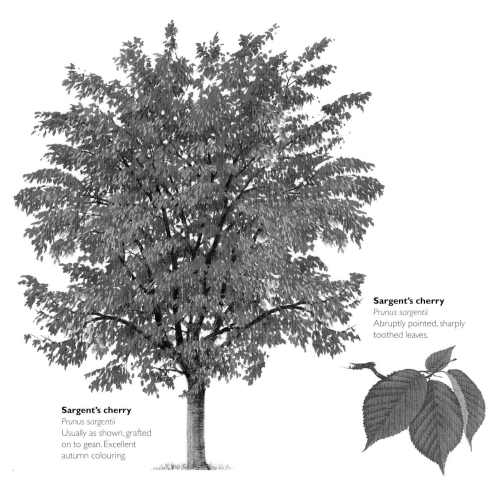

Sargent's cherry
Prunus sargentii
Abruptly pointed, sharply
toothed leaves.

Sargent's cherry
Prunus sargentii
Usually as shown, grafted
on to gean. Excellent
autumn colouring.

been cultivated in many countries for hundreds of years and now has dozens of varieties — some are grown for their luscious fruits, others for the beauty of their flowers.

It is a small, bushy tree, up to 8m (25ft) tall, and the original wild stock has long lanceolate pointed leaves, 7–15cm (3–6in) long, finely toothed, with a glandular stalk about 1.5cm (½in) long. The rose-pink flowers, 2.5–4cm (1–1½in) across, make a wonderful show in spring, and the fruit is globose, 5–8cm (2–3in) in diameter, covered with velvety down, with a shallow groove on one side. When ripe, they are golden suffused with red and exceedingly

sweet and juicy. The stone is grooved and very hard.

Some of the cultivated varieties are very beautiful: 'Alba' and 'Alboplena', with single and double white flowers respectively; 'Russell's Red', with double crimson flowers; 'Klara Mayer', with double pink flowers; 'Aurora', with dense clusters of double rose-pink flowers with fringed petals; and 'Pendula', an attractive weeping form, with masses of white flowers.

Sargent's cherry (*Prunus sargentii*)

The great mountain cherry, seen so wonderfully on the slopes of Fujiyama, Japan, is widely used in many countries.

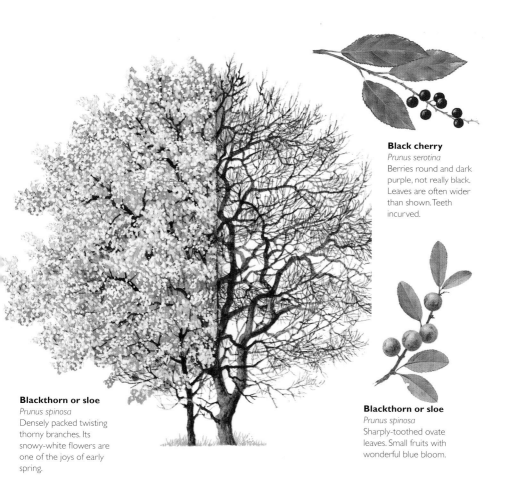

Black cherry
Prunus serotina
Berries round and dark
purple, not really black.
Leaves are often wider
than shown. Teeth
incurved.

Blackthorn or sloe
Prunus spinosa
Densely packed twisting
thorny branches. Its
snowy-white flowers are
one of the joys of early
spring.

Blackthorn or sloe
Prunus spinosa
Sharply-toothed ovate
leaves. Small fruits with
wonderful blue bloom.

It is a large, fast-growing tree, up to 25m (80ft), with reddish young leaves and bunches of large pink flowers on wide-angled branches. The tree gives fine red and gold autumn colours.

'Accolade', a cross between *Prunus sargentii* and *P. subhirtella*, has semi-double pink flowers with fringed petals. It has a broad open crown and flowers in bunches all the way up the branches, opening before the leaves appear.

Prunus × schmittii

The hybrid *Prunus × schmittii* is a good narrow-form tree, with pale pink flowers and the special feature of beautiful, dark, red-brown bark with horizontal stripes.

Black or rum cherry *(Prunus serotina)*

This species is very like the bird cherry *(Prunus padus)* but differs as follows: the flower spikes are more upright in the black cherry than the bird cherry, the leaves are very glossy dark green, and the fruits are red, turning dark purple rather than black, as in bird cherry.

Blackthorn or sloe *(Prunus spinosa)*

This is the commonest wild plum. It is a very aggressive bush or small tree that quickly spreads by sucker growth to form an impenetrable thicket armed with sharp black thorns and held together by

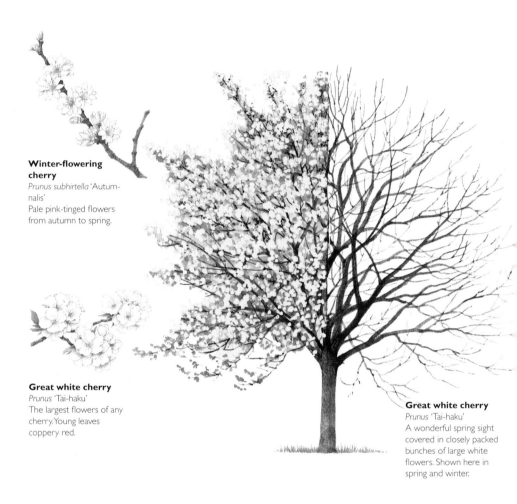

Winter-flowering cherry
Prunus subhirtella 'Autumnalis'
Pale pink-tinged flowers from autumn to spring.

Great white cherry
Prunus 'Tai-haku'
The largest flowers of any cherry. Young leaves coppery red.

Great white cherry
Prunus 'Tai-haku'
A wonderful spring sight covered in closely packed bunches of large white flowers. Shown here in spring and winter.

its crooked interlacing branches. Native to Europe and northern Asia, it will grow to a maximum of about 7m (22ft) but more usually around 4m (12ft), and is a wonderful sight in spring, when its bare black twigs are covered with masses of pure white flowers, each 1.5cm (½in) across. The ovate, sharply toothed leaves, 2–4cm (¾–1½in) long, turn a fawny gold in autumn. The bark on old stems is blackish grey, breaking away in small flakes, with a tendency to horizontal markings.

The fruit, known as a 'sloe', is about 1.5cm (½in) in diameter, blue-black and covered with a very beautiful bloom when ripe. It is harshly sour but is used for making sloe-gin, sloe-wine and jelly.

Winter-flowering cherry
(*Prunus subhirtella* 'Autumnalis')
This cultivar of *Prunus subhirtella* has semi-double, pink-tinged white flowers from mid-autumn to early spring.

Great white cherry (*Prunus* 'Tai-haku')
This is probably the finest of all the whites, and is a magnificent sight in spring, with its masses of large single flowers and rich copper-red young leaves. It is wide-growing and vigorous, reaching 12m (40ft) high.

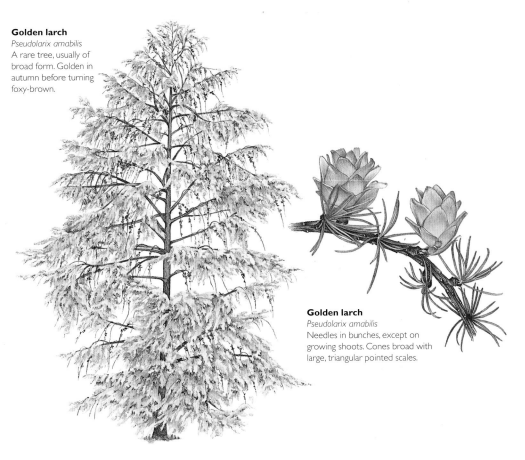

Golden larch
Pseudolarix amabilis
A rare tree, usually of
broad form. Golden in
autumn before turning
foxy-brown.

Golden larch
Pseudolarix amabilis
Needles in bunches, except on
growing shoots. Cones broad with
large, triangular pointed scales.

Golden Larch (*Pseudolarix amabilis*)

This is a genus of one species of coniferous tree from the forests of China, grown for its outstanding autumn foliage.

Golden larch (*Pseudolarix amabilis*)
This is not a true larch (*Larix*) but it is very close indeed, having the same sort of needle arrangement and being deciduous. But the cones are quite different, bluish green at first, turning to light brown as they ripen, up to 4.5 x 4.5cm (1¾ x 1¾in) with large, triangular, acute-pointed leathery scales and whitish seeds with long 3cm/ 1¼in) pointed wings.

Unlike true larches, golden larch cones fall off when ripe; they often only crop every second year.

The needles are long, 3–7cm (1¼–3in), and the bunches are borne on curved spurs, thickest at the tips. Because they turn golden in autumn the native name for the tree is 'ching-sung', meaning 'golden pine'.

The male and female flowers are very small and borne on separate branches. The tree is broadly conic with long level branches and in China reaches to 40m (130ft) but is often dwarfed by pruning for ornamental effect. The wood is very good but the species is too rare to be cut for timber.

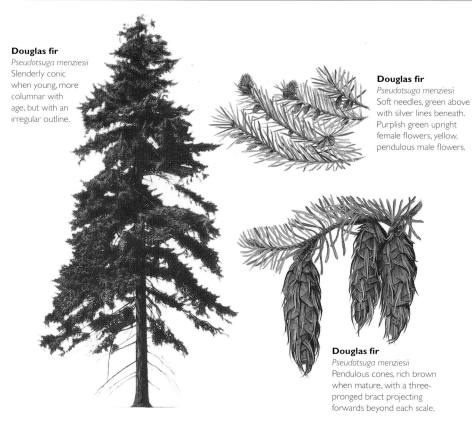

Douglas fir
Pseudotsuga menziesii
Slenderly conic
when young, more
columnar with
age, but with an
irregular outline.

Douglas fir
Pseudotsuga menziesii
Soft needles, green above
with silver lines beneath.
Purplish green upright
female flowers, yellow,
pendulous male flowers.

Douglas fir
Pseudotsuga menziesii
Pendulous cones, rich brown
when mature, with a three-
pronged bract projecting
forwards beyond each scale.

Douglas Fir (*Pseudotsuga menziesii*)

There are about six to eight evergreen, coniferous trees in the genus *Pseudotsuga*, the most important of which is *P. menziesii*.

Douglas fir *(Pseudotsuga menziesii)*
Douglas fir is native from the Alaskan border through the western seaboard to Mexico. It is one of the world's tallest trees and is fast growing, often making annual shoots of 1–2m (3–6ft).

The needles are arranged in two loose ranks, dark green above with two silvery white bands on the lower surface; when crushed they emit a strong fragrance. The buds are reddish brown and spindle-shaped. Male flowers are in blunt conic clusters on the underside of the twigs, pink at first then golden as pollen is shed; female flowers are at the side of the shoots and turn upwards to form erect, crimson, cone-like tufts turning green later. The cones are pendulous, up to 8 x 2.5cm (3 x 1in) long, light brown and with trident bracts protruding between the cone scales. The small winged seeds are a lighter brown on one side than the other. On old trees, the bark is very rugged and fissured but on young trees, and near the top of older ones, it is smooth except for numerous blisters.

Young trees grown in the open are narrowly conical with long slender leading shoots, but mature trees, though still fairly slender for their height, become rather flatter at the top and the heavy lower branches droop markedly.

Caucasian wing nut
Pterocarya fraxinifolia
Seed chains up to 45cm
(18in) long. Leaves are
even longer and with
overlapping leaflets.

Caucasian wing nut
Pterocarya fraxinifolia
A broad-crowned tree, shown here
in summer, with a short or
sometimes no bole at all.

Wing nuts (*Pterocarya*)

The wing nuts belong to the walnut family (Juglandaceae) and the twigs have the same type of chambered pith. They have large pinnate leaves, sometimes up to 60cm (24in) long, the toothed leaflets varying from 5 to 27 in number. The small male and female flowers are on separate catkins, the female ones much longer than the male. Wing nuts are a very striking sight when they are festooned with their long greenish yellow catkins.

Caucasian wingnut
(Pterocarya fraxinifolia)
This is the most widely used species and the largest growing, reaching up to 30m (100ft). Its female catkins lengthen up to as much as 50cm (20in) before the autumn. The leaves have from 9 to 27 crowded overlapping leaflets, shiny green above and paler beneath.

Chinese wing nut
(Pterocarya paliuris)
This Chinese species has remarkable circular winged seeds, up to 7cm (3in) in diameter, looking like little cymbals.

Pterocarya x rehderana
This hybrid wingnut (a cross between *Pterocarya caucasica* and *P. stenoptera*) is very ornamental with prolific catkins.

Japanese wing nut
(Pterocarya rhoifolia)
This is one of the finest trees in the Mt Hakkoda area, Japan, where it reaches 30m (100ft) in height and grows to an elevation of 1,220m (4,000ft).

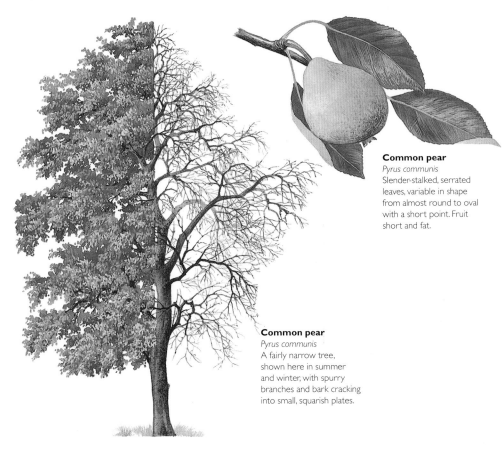

Common pear
Pyrus communis
Slender-stalked, serrated
leaves, variable in shape
from almost round to oval
with a short point. Fruit
short and fat.

Common pear
Pyrus communis
A fairly narrow tree,
shown here in summer
and winter, with spurry
branches and bark cracking
into small, squarish plates.

Pears (*Pyrus*)

A group of about 20 species in the north temperate region character-ized by flowers in umbel-like corymbs and fruits with a certain 'gritty' texture, especially when unripe. A small selection of the wild and ornamental species will be considered here, omitting the large number of hybrids and cultivars pro-duced for marketing the fruits. Unlike apples, pears have only a minimal depression at the point where the stalk joins the fruit.

Common pear (*Pyrus communis*)
Native to Europe and western Asia, a tall, fairly narrow tree with a rounded top when mature and branches that tend to ascend first and then bend over towards the end; this grows up to 18m (60ft), with dark bark cracking into squarish plates.

The leaves are ovate to elliptic, 5–8cm (2–3in) long, on stalks 2–4cm (¾–1½in) long; they are finely crenate, dark shiny green above, and paler beneath. The branches have many short stiff spurs, sometimes spiny. Masses of white flowers emerge before the leaves are fully out, 2–3.5cm (¾–1½in) across, and grouped in little bunches. The fruit is small, 2.5–5cm (1–2in) long, and is sometimes rather round.

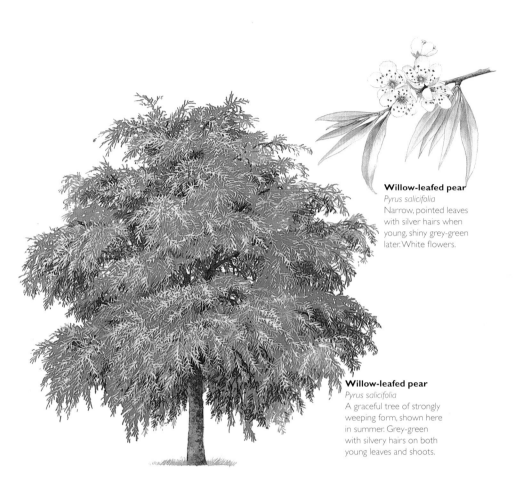

Willow-leafed pear
Pyrus salicifolia
Narrow, pointed leaves
with silver hairs when
young, shiny grey-green
later. White flowers.

Willow-leafed pear
Pyrus salicifolia
A graceful tree of strongly
weeping form, shown here
in summer. Grey-green
with silvery hairs on both
young leaves and shoots.

Mediterranean pear *(Pyrus nivalis)*
Another European species, this is grown
in France for its fruit and in many countries for its abundant pure white flowers
in spring, and narrow oval leaves that
when young are coated with pure white
down and look most striking.

Willow-leafed pear *(Pyrus salicifolia)*
This very ornamental small tree, from
Europe and western Asia, grows to
approximately 9m (28ft), with ascending
branches markedly pendulous at the end,
and a rounded crown. The more weeping
types are often named as 'Pendula'. It has
beautiful silver-green, willow-like leaves,

tapered at both ends and with lots of
white hairy down, especially when
young. The small pure white flowers are
closely packed in small clusters, the
calyx and flower stems covered in white
wool. Fruits are small, typically pear-
shaped, and 2.5–3.5cm (1–1½in) long.

Sand pear *(Pyrus sinensis)*
Native to northern Asia and planted in
China and Japan for its quite large fruits
— up to 12cm (5in) long and very variable in both colour and form, usually
speckled yellow and brown but sometimes marked with red or almost pure
yellow; they tend to be sour-tasting.

California live oak
Quercus agrifolia
Bristle-toothed, dark green
leaves; pointed acorns set
in deep cups.

White oak
Quercus alba
Shown here in summer,
this is a superb tree with
purple autumn colours.

Oaks (*Quercus*)

There are over 300 species of ever-green or deciduous oak in the north-ern temperate regions, as well as many hybrids and clones. Most oak species share the following characteristics. They all have seeds in the form of acorns but these vary greatly in size, shape and form of the cups. The buds are usually in clus-ters, often with several about the same size, resulting in the numbers of large irregular branches that give most oaks their characteristic rugged crowns. The male flowers develop in the form of drooping catkins, with fewer females, on short stalks, erect above the males.

California live oak *(Quercus agrifolia)*
This evergreen species strongly resembles Holm oak *(Quercus ilex, see opposite)*.

White oak *(Quercus alba)*
This magnificent tree, up to 45m (150ft) tall, from eastern and central USA, is a major species over large areas of Ameri-can forests. The large deciduous leaves, 8–12cm (3–5in) broad x 16–20cm (6–8in) long, are narrow sharply towards the stalk, and have four to six pairs of round-ended lobes glossy green above, whitish underneath, turning to a purple colour in the autumn. The acorns are about 2cm (¾in) long in shallow cups.

White oak
Quercus alba
Deeply lobed, pale green leaves.

Holm oak
Quercus ilex
Glossy evergreen leaves with
white hairy undersides;
greenish white acorn cups.

Mirbecks oak *(Quercus canariensis* syn. *Q. mirbeckii)*

A handsome tree native to North Africa and Spain, up to 30m (100ft) tall. It is partly evergreen, often with some green and some brown leaves in winter. Oblong-obovate leaves vary in size from 8–20cm x 5–11cm (3–8in x 2–4½in), with 6 to 12 pairs of small pointed lobes and red stalks.

Chestnut-leaved oak
(Quercus castaneifolia)

This deciduous oak is from Iran and the Caucasus, with fat acorns, 2cm (¾in) across, and less spiny-edged leaves.

Scarlet oak *(Quercus coccinea)*

A deciduous American species, sometimes confused with red oak *(Quercus rubra)*, though scarlet oak is smaller, with smaller leaves on longer stalks with about three widely spaced, pointed lobes cut in nearly to the midrib, and more regular deep red autumn colouring. The small acorns develop in shallow, large-scaled cups.

Holm oak *(Quercus ilex)*

This southern European tree is one of the most widely used evergreen oaks and grows up to 30m (100ft), with a broad-domed, very dense crown and usually large, low branches. Its bark is blackish

Sessile oak
Quercus petraea
Acorns are stalkless; leaves
are borne on definite
stalks.

Willow oak
Quercus phellos
Long narrow leaves mimic
those of the willow tree;
small brown acorns.

Chestnut oak
Quercus prinus
Mid-green leaves mimic
those of the sweet
chestnut tree.

brown and shallowly fissured. The terminal buds have some curled whiskers and the leaves are dense on the twigs; they may be lanceolate or oval, entire or toothed, wavy-edged or flat and 3–12cm (1¼–5in) long. The tree is a dull gold when the new leaves emerge, but otherwise dark green. The small acorns, 1.5–2cm (½–¾in) long, are often half-enclosed in the cup of felted scales.

Burr oak

(Quercus macrocarpa)

This is a large, widely distributed North American deciduous species that may reach 52m (170ft). It has broadly ovate,

chestnut-brown acorns, finely pubescent at the apex, and set in cups with a fringe of hairs round the top, and pointed, raised scales.

Sessile or durmast oak

(Quercus petraea syn. Q. sessiliflora)

This has much the same native distribution as the common oak (*Quercus robur*), but the leaves are flatter, more leathery, less bunched, and have five to nine pairs of rounded, less deeply cut lobes, on leaf stalks 1–2cm (½–¾in) long; the acorns have no stalks.

Willow oak *(Quercus phellos)*

Up to 30m (100ft) tall from eastern USA,

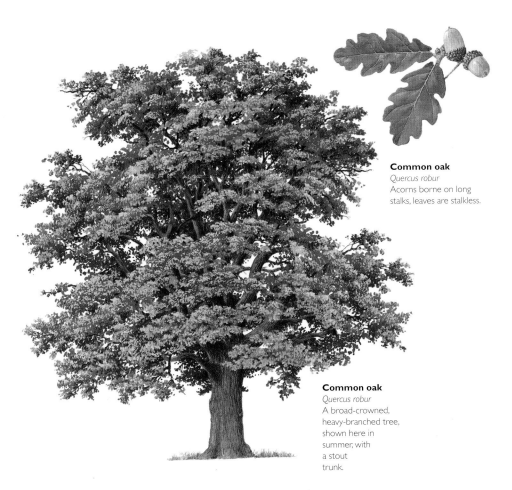

Common oak
Quercus robur
Acorns borne on long
stalks, leaves are stalkless.

Common oak
Quercus robur
A broad-crowned,
heavy-branched tree,
shown here in
summer, with
a stout
trunk.

with ascending branches and a domed crown. It has narrow, entire, willow-like deciduous leaves, 5–12cm (2–5in) long and 1.5–2cm (½–¾in) wide, pointed at both ends, which turn pale-yellow in autumn. Its small acorns, about 1cm (½in) long have shallow cups.

Chestnut or tanbark oak
(Quercus prinus)

A handsome, round-headed tree, up to 30m (100ft) tall, this is native to central and southern USA. The leaves, 10–18cm (4–7in) long x 4–8cm (1½–3in) wide, resemble those of sweet chestnut (*Castanea*) but the lobes are more rounded and less sharply pointed, with 10 to 14 parallel veins, and maturing to rich crimson colours in autumn; the ovoid acorns are 2.5–3.5cm (1–1½in) long.

Common or pedunculate oak
(Quercus robur syn. Q. pedunculata)

A large deciduous tree, up to 37m (125ft) tall, native to Europe, the Caucasus, Asia Minor and North Africa, this species is long living. It has a large, spreading crown, often wider than tall, with massive twisting branches. The leaves have a somewhat wavy surface, often bunched together, auricled at the base, oblong-obovate, 8–12cm (3–5in) long, with four

Cork oak
Quercus suber
Glossy leaves with pale green undersides and prickles at tips of veins.

Red oak
Quercus rubra
Autumn leaves and large acorns set in shallow cups.

Red oak
Quercus rubra
Striking autumn coloration before losing its leaves.

to six pairs of rounded lobes and a very short stalk, 3–7mm long (⅛–¼in). The flowers appear in mid- to late spring, the males in green clusters on a hanging stalk, 5–7cm (2–3in) long, the females on short erect stalks above the male catkins. The acorns, 2–4cm (¾–1½in) long, often develop in pairs, with 3–7cm (1¼–3in) stalks, and shallow cups.

Red oak *(Quercus rubra* syn. *Q. borealis)*

Native and widespread in Canada and northeastern USA, red oak grows to 40m (130ft) tall. The large, oblong deciduous leaves, 12–24cm (5–10in) long, with acute points on the variable-sized lobes, start bright yellow in spring, usually becoming deep red in the autumn, but this is variable. It is fast-growing, with annual shoots up to 2m (6ft).

Cork oak *(Quercus suber)*

The thick soft outer bark of this medium-sized tree from southern Europe and North Africa is still the world's main source of cork. Soon after stripping, the trunks turn a rich red colour. The hard, oblong-ovate evergreen leaves are lustrous dark green above with whitish pubescence below, the margins wavy with shallow spine-tipped lobes.

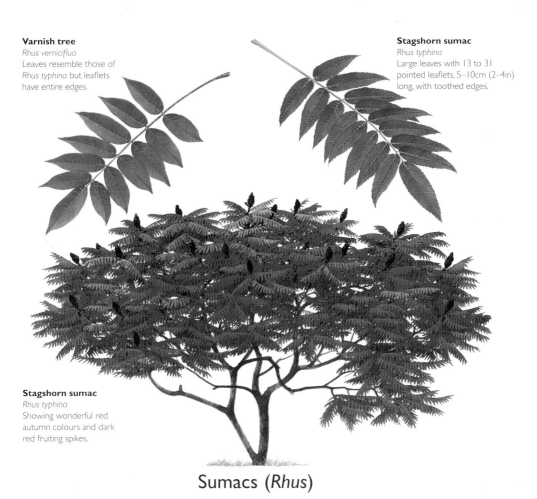

Varnish tree
Rhus verniciflua
Leaves resemble those of
Rhus typhina but leaflets
have entire edges.

Stagshorn sumac
Rhus typhina
Large leaves with 13 to 31
pointed leaflets, 5–10cm (2–4in)
long, with toothed edges.

Stagshorn sumac
Rhus typhina
Showing wonderful red
autumn colours and dark
red fruiting spikes.

Sumacs (*Rhus*)

This genus of some 150 species belongs to the great cashew family, Anacardiaceae. Its leaves may be large and pinnate or simple, some deciduous, some evergreen, and several rather poisonous, particularly the poison ivy (*Rhus toxicodendron*) of the eastern USA.

Stagshorn sumac (*Rhus typhina*)

This small, flat-topped deciduous tree from North America has very thick twigs that are covered with red-brown hairs. The large pinnate leaves, hairy when young, are 25–60cm (10–24in) long, with pointed, lanceolate, toothed leaflets; in autumn, they turn flaming orange, red and purple. Male and female flowers are on separate trees, in spikes or panicles made up of many tiny flowers; the male panicles are lax, reddish green and up to 30cm (12in) tall, the female ones denser and smaller, turning later to a red hairy 'candle-flame' of seeds, which remain on the tree long after leaf fall. The stems contain an acrid, milky sap.

Varnish tree (*Rhus verniciflua*)

This attractive small tree, up to 15m (50ft) tall, comes from China, Japan and the Himalayas. Its leaves have entire margins. The yellowish white flowers are tiny and borne in large loose panicles.

Locust tree
Robinia pseudoacacia
Delicate pinnate leaves.
Racemes of hanging white
flowers.

Locust tree
Robinia pseudoacacia
Open-crowned with
twisting branches and
rough, deeply ridged bark.

Locust Tree (*Robinia pseudoacacia*)

Locust is a name often loosely applied to a number of different trees and shrubs. The one considered here belongs to the genus *Robinia*, but there are some locusts classified under other genera, such as *Ceratonia* and *Gleditsia*. There are about 20 species in the genus *Robinia*, all of which are from North America and Mexico.

Locust tree or false acacia
(*Robinia pseudoacacia*)

This fine tree from eastern USA grows to about 30m (100ft), with a rough open crown broadest at the top, deeply ridged and fissured bark, alternate pinnate leaves, 15–20cm (6–8in) long, with 11 to 19 oval entire leaflets, each with a tiny spine on its rounded end, and short paired spines at each bud, making the twigs prickly. The scented white flowers grow in racemes, 10–20cm (4–8in) long, and fairly narrow seed-pods, 5–10cm (2–4in) long, ripen to dark brown with black seeds. Unfortunately, the branches split away from the trunk rather easily, often spoiling the shape of the tree.

There are many cultivars of this tree, offering different coloured flowers, golden leaves, thornless twigs, and contorted or dwarf forms.

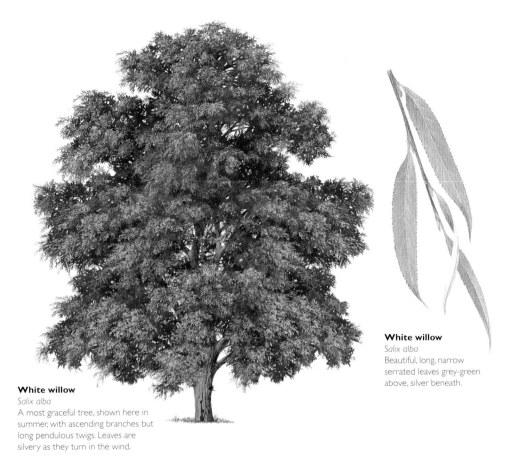

White willow
Salix alba
A most graceful tree, shown here in summer, with ascending branches but long pendulous twigs. Leaves are silvery as they turn in the wind.

White willow
Salix alba
Beautiful, long, narrow serrated leaves grey-green above, silver beneath.

Willows (*Salix*)

This genus with over 300 species has the widest geographical distribution of any tree — right across the northern hemisphere and down into South America and South Africa. Their identification has been greatly complicated by frequent hybrids and only a few of the main examples can be considered here.

Willows vary from creeping pioneer species to tall trees, some of which yield valuable timber, but many of them are shrubby with no marked central trunk. The buds of all willows are enclosed in a single rounded scale and, with rare exceptions, every tree is either wholly male or wholly female. The open female catkins, with their whitish stigmas, are usually silvery green, while the males have golden anthers. The seeds are minute, each bearing a mass of fluffy white hairs, and will only germinate on damp soil; this explains why willows only spread along watersides or on marshes. In most species the leaves are long, narrow and alternate.

White willow (*Salix alba*)
This tree is similar in size and distribution to the crack willow (*Salix fragilis*) but has a denser crown, more pendulous long, slender twigs, male catkins 4–6cm

153

Cricket bat willow
Salix alba 'Coerulea'
Long, narrow, blue-grey
green leaves.

Cricket bat willow
Salix alba 'Coerulea'
Conic, rather narrow and
upright tree, shown here in
summer.

(1½–2½in) and females 4–7cm (1½–3in). The leaves are shorter, closer together and set more irregularly on the twigs, bluer green above and much whiter beneath.

'Chermesina' (Scarlet willow or coralbark willow), also sometimes known as 'Chrysostella' or 'Britzensis', is a special cultivar of *Salix alba*, with orange-scarlet twigs, and is very conspicuous and beautiful in winter.

'Coerulea' (cricket bat or blue willow) is another *Salix alba* cultivar which, together with special hybrids and clones from it, is specially grown to provide top-class cricket bats. It is of conic upright form, has slender purple shoots, bluish grey-green leaves, and a narrow crown.

Weeping willow *(Salix babylonica)*
The original weeping willow is *Salix babylonica*, a native of China and probably not the tree referred to in the Bible; it is used much less often than the larger, more vigorous hybrid, with much yellower twigs, called *Salix vitellina* var. *pendula* (syns. *S.* 'Tristis' and *S.* 'Chrysocoma'), a cross between *S. vitellina* and *S. babylonica*.

All the weeping willows are distinguished by cascades of beautiful pendu-

Weeping willow
Salix babylonica
The very graceful original weeping species.

Goat willow
Salix caprea
Thick, usually broad leaves. Ripe seeds covered in white fluff.

lous slender shoots, often hanging to touch the water beneath.

Goat willow, sallow or pussy willow (Salix caprea)

This bushy small tree is native to Europe and northern Asia. It is well known and much loved for its heavy crop of beautiful short fat catkins in early spring, all silky silver at first, then the males turning golden-yellow and the females silvery green. When the seeds are ripe, the catkins are like balls of white fluff. The leaves vary in size and shape — anything from small lanceolate, 3–4cm (1¼–1½in) long, to large, broadly rounded, 6cm (2½in) across, or oblong, up to 9cm (3½in) long. In general, the leaves are grey-green, serrate or entire, often wrinkled and on short red stalks. The shoots on old trees are short and knobbly. If not cut back, this tree will grow up to 12m (40ft) tall on favourable wet sites, but will survive on very poor rough ground.

Crack willow (Salix fragilis)

Common and with a wide range across Europe, western Siberia, and extending into Iran, this species grows to 30m (100ft) tall, with long upswept branches, heavy and twisted on old trees, which are broadly domed and often become

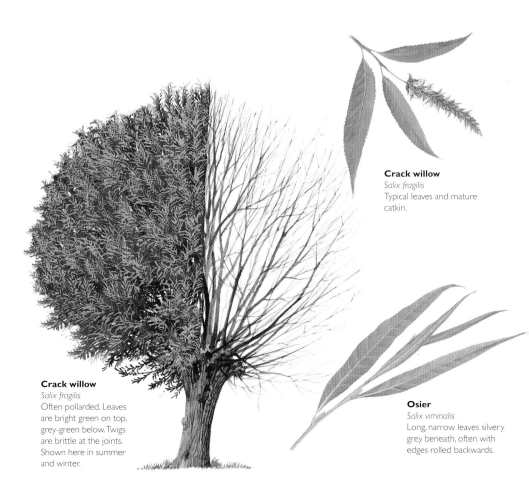

Crack willow
Salix fragilis
Typical leaves and mature catkin.

Crack willow
Salix fragilis
Often pollarded. Leaves are bright green on top, grey-green below. Twigs are brittle at the joints. Shown here in summer and winter.

Osier
Salix viminalis
Long, narrow leaves silvery grey beneath, often with edges rolled backwards.

slanted. The twigs snap off very easily at the base: hence the name 'crack' willow.

The male catkins are yellow, 2–5cm (¾–2in), the females pale green, 6–10cm (2½–4in). The narrow lanceolate leaves, 10–18cm (4–7in) long, are usually finely tapered, glossy green above and grey-green beneath, and hang evenly on the twigs. The bark on old trees is very rugged, deeply furrowed, and tends to flake off.

Contorted willow
(Salix matsudana 'Tortuosa')
A cultivar of the Japanese tree *Salix matsudana*, this tree has amazingly con-torted branches, twigs and leaves.

Osier willows
(Salix viminalis cultivars)
A most important group of special clones and hybrids, nearly all derived from the common osier (*Salix viminalis*). They are specifically grown and harvested for the basket and willow-weaving trade.

In general, osier leaves are narrower than those of most willows, silvery grey and often hairy beneath, varying in length from 7–25cm (3–10in). The shoots vary over a whole range of colours — red, yellow, purple, brown, green, cream, to almost black.

Common elder
Sambucus nigra
Beautiful glossy black
berries much used for
culinary and medicinal
purposes.

Pacific red elder
Sambucus callicarpa
Scarlet berries in a panicle
rather than in a flat umbel.

Elders (*Sambucus*)

The elders, mainly from America and Europe, are an interesting and useful little group of deciduous shrubs and small trees, characterized by: opposite pinnate leaves always having an odd number, from 3 to 11, of toothed leaflets; young shoots lined with soft pith; and clusters of small white, or yellowish white flowers and berries varying from black to blue or red.

Pacific red elder
(*Sambucus callicarpa*)

This elder has scarlet berries that are borne in a fairly long panicle rather than in a flat umbel.

American elder
(*Sambucus canadensis*)

Closely allied to the common elder (*Sambucus nigra*), the eastern American elder is smaller, seldom more than 4m (12ft) high. Its leaves usually have more leaflets, the flower heads are not so flat, and the berries are dark purple when ripe instead of black.

Common elder (*Sambucus nigra*)

Native to Europe, this is an amazingly hardy species, succeeding even on very poor or very alkaline soils, immune to rabbit damage, and tolerant of smoke and fumes, severe exposure and heavy

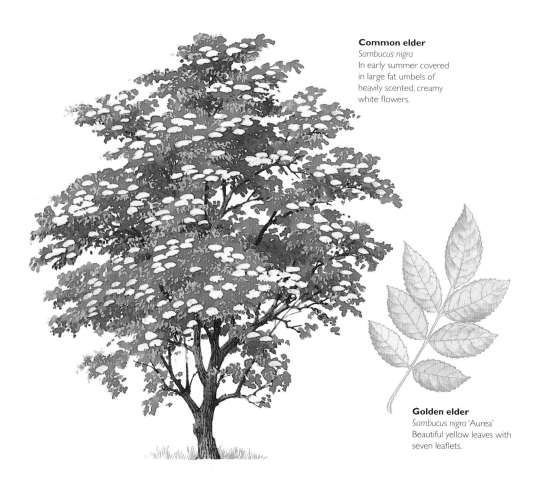

Common elder
Sambucus nigra
In early summer covered
in large fat umbels of
heavily scented, creamy
white flowers.

Golden elder
Sambucus nigra 'Aurea'
Beautiful yellow leaves with
seven leaflets.

shade. The berries and/or the flowers are used for making wine, cough syrup and elderflower water.

In hedges, elder is usually cut back and forms a bush, but left alone it will make a small tree up to 10m (30ft) high. The opposite leaves, 10–25cm (4–10in) long, have three to seven toothed leaflets. The white flowers occur in flat umbels, 10–20cm (4–8in) across. Both the leaves and flowers emit a strong smell, especially when crushed. On young twigs the bark has conspicuous lenticels, while on old trunks it has deep fissures.

There are many attractive cultivars,

such as 'Aurea' (golden elder), with attractive yellow leaves with seven leaflets. There are also variegated and pink-flowered kinds.

Red-berried elder

(Sambucus racemosa)

Native to Europe, Asia Minor, northern China and Siberia, this species forms a growing shrub, only up to 4m (12ft) high. Its yellowish white flowers are in pyramidal panicles, and the bright red berries ripen in summer, much earlier than in common elder (*Sambucus nigra*). There are cut-leaved, gold-leaved, white- and pink-flowered cultivars.

Sassafras
Sassafras albidum
A narrow tree with
twisting, upswept branches
and splendid autumn
colours.

Sassafras
Sassafras albidum
Strongly aromatic leaves
very variable in shape but
mostly three-lobed.

Sassafras (*Sassafras albidum*)

This genus consists of a very small group of only three species closely related to the true laurels. They are grown for their majestic habit and glossy foliage. Only the common sassafras (*Sassafras albidum*) is at all well known.

Common sassafras

(*Sassafras albidum* syn. *S. officinale*)

An interesting eastern American species growing to 30m (100ft) tall, with upswept twisting branches and grey bark with irregular dark fissures. Its thin, mid-green leaves are remarkable for varying greatly in size and shape, even on the same branch, from entire simple ovals to regular three-lobed form or even lop-sided two-lobed shapes, up to 18 x 8cm (7 x 3in) on short, often red stalks; they display brilliant yellow and red autumn colours. The small yellowish green flowers, about 8mm (⅜in) across, are in racemes 3–6cm (1¼–2½in) long, male and female usually on separate trees; they are not very beautiful or conspicuous, and the fruit is only a small bluish black ovoid shape, about 1cm (½in) long.

The whole tree is very aromatic; the bark and roots are sometimes used to brew a kind of tea, and oil of sassafras is used for soaps and liniments.

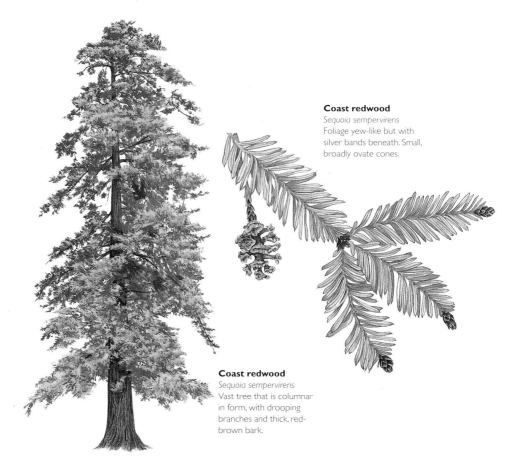

Coast redwood
Sequoia sempervirens
Foliage yew-like but with silver bands beneath. Small, broadly ovate cones.

Coast redwood
Sequoia sempervirens
Vast tree that is columnar in form, with drooping branches and thick, red-brown bark.

Coast Redwood (*Sequoia sempervirens*)

This is a genus of one species of very tall tree, closely related to the giant sequoia (*Sequoiadendron giganteum*, see opposite), but less hardy.

Coast redwood or Californian redwood (*Sequoia sempervirens*)

Apart from its immense size (it can reach 112m/365ft, but usually grows to about 20–30m/70–100ft), one of the special features of this tree is its soft, fibrous, red-brown bark, which may become 40cm (16in) thick on old trees, and is usually deeply fissured into rough-edged inter-twining ridges. Its foliage is very like that of yew (*Taxus*), with linear, sharp-pointed leaves, 1.5–2cm (½–¾in) long, dark green above but with two whitish bands below that are missing in yew. The yellow male flowers occur on the ends of small shoots, while the female flowers are oval, greenish and formed of 14 to 20 bracts tipped with short points. The cones are about 2cm (¾in) long, and grow on slender stalks. They are initially oval-round with wrinkled scales and green but turning brown or brownish. The seeds are narrowly winged and tiny.

'Adpressa', a smaller cultivar at 20m (70ft), has creamy white shoots, shorter, closely packed leaves, and smaller cones.

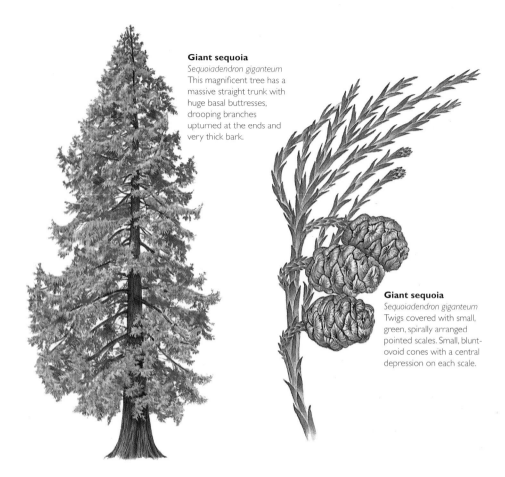

Giant sequoia
Sequoiadendron giganteum
This magnificent tree has a massive straight trunk with huge basal buttresses, drooping branches upturned at the ends and very thick bark.

Giant sequoia
Sequoiadendron giganteum
Twigs covered with small, green, spirally arranged pointed scales. Small, blunt-ovoid cones with a central depression on each scale.

Giant Sequoia (*Sequoiadendron giganteum*)

A vast tree, closely related to the coast redwood (*Sequoia sempervirens, see opposite*). Is is also one of the oldest living things on earth, some specimens having lived to 4,000 years.

Giant sequoia
(*Sequoiadendron giganteum*)

The giant sequoias do not quite reach the heights of the coast redwood, but there are many between 60 and 90m (200 and 300ft), and they easily beat them on girth. The foliage differs from that of the coast redwood, and consists of spirally arranged, scale-like needles, 4–7mm (⅙–⅛in), grey-green at the base, deep green above. The twigs are upright at the branch ends, pendulous and out-turned elsewhere; the heavy lower branches droop but are upswept again towards the tips. Male flowers occur as little yellow beads, while the ovoid female flowers are erect on pinkish yellow stalks. The green cones are up to 8 x 5cm (3 x 2in) and bluntly ovoid with flat, diamond-shaped scales, each with a central depression. The flat-winged seeds are small.

The bark is not quite such a bright red as that of the coast redwood, but is just as soft and even thicker — it can be 50cm (20in) on old trees.

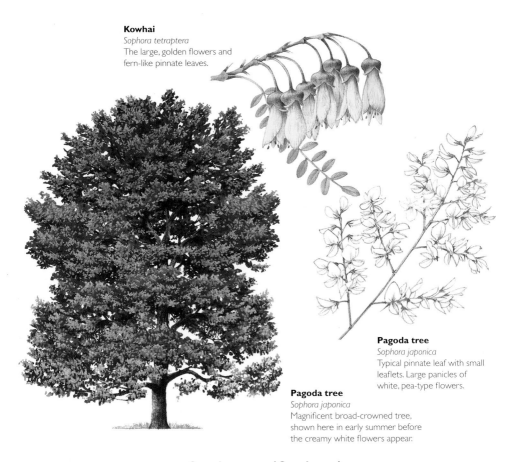

Kowhai
Sophora tetraptera
The large, golden flowers and fern-like pinnate leaves.

Pagoda tree
Sophora japonica
Typical pinnate leaf with small leaflets. Large panicles of white, pea-type flowers.

Pagoda tree
Sophora japonica
Magnificent broad-crowned tree, shown here in early summer before the creamy white flowers appear.

Sophoras (*Sophora*)

Belonging to the great pea family, Leguminosae, there are about 20 sophora tree species.

Pagoda or scholar's tree
(Sophora japonica)
Native to China and Korea, this splendid deciduous tree reaches 25m (80ft) high. It is like *Robinia* but is wider and more rounded, with massive contorted branches, pinnate alternate leaves, 15–25cm (6–10in) long, with 9 to 15 entire pointed, narrowly ovate leaflets, 3–5cm (1¼–2in) long. The late-summer flowers, which do not appear for the first 30 years, are in terminal panicles, 15–25cm (6–10in) long, with pubescent stems and creamy white flowers, sometimes almost yellow. The seed-pods are small, 5–10cm (2–4in) long. Mature bark is grey-brown and corrugated.

Kowhai *(Sophora tetraptera)*
This is a very beautiful New Zealand tree, up to 15m (50ft) tall, with slender zig-zag branches. It has smaller, more fern-like leaves than pagoda tree (*Sophora japonica*), with a variable number of leaflets, from 7 to 70. The flowers are tubular, 3–5cm (1¼–2in) long, come out in late spring, and are golden-yellow; seed-pods are 5–20cm (2–8in) long with four wings.

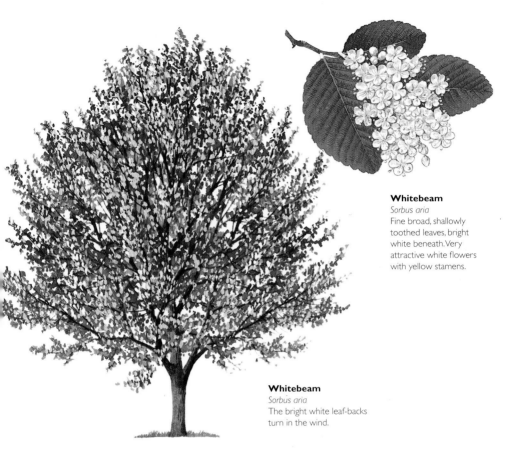

Whitebeam
Sorbus aria
Fine broad, shallowly
toothed leaves, bright
white beneath. Very
attractive white flowers
with yellow stamens.

Whitebeam
Sorbus aria
The bright white leaf-backs
turn in the wind.

Whitebeams, Rowans and Service Trees (*Sorbus*)

This branch of the great Rosaceae family contains about 80 northern temperate species ranging from Scotland to the Himalayas and down to Mexico, mostly with attractive berries and pinnate leaves.

Whitebeam *(Sorbus aria)*

This very beautiful European tree thrives in chalk and limestone soils; its unique feature is its wonderful oval, doubly toothed leaves, up to 9 x 5cm (3½ x 2in), with marked veins, bright green above but covered with silver down beneath. In spring the buds open into pure white spikes. The heavily scented flowers are creamy white, about 1.5cm (½in) across, and in corymbs about 6–9cm (2½–3½in) in diameter; the bright red berries are 1cm (½in) long, roundish oval, contrasting with the white-backed leaves. In autumn the leaves are a pinkish shade on the back when they fall. The bark is smooth and light grey between long irregular fissures.

Rowan or mountain ash
(Sorbus aucuparia)

Spread widely over Europe and also in parts of Asia and North Africa, this very hardy, beautiful little tree occasionally reaches 20m (70ft) but usually only

Rowan
Sorbus aucuparia
A most attractive little tree in flower in late spring or loaded with scarlet berries in late summer, as here.

Rowan
Sorbus aucuparia
Pinnate leaves and glorious red berries.

Sargent's rowan
Sorbus sargentiana
A Chinese species with large pinnate leaves that give rich red autumn colours.

about 10m (30ft). It is famous for its masses of striking orange-red berries, up to 1cm (½in) across, in dense bunches. It has an irregular shaped crown, strongly ascending branches and steely-grey bark, smooth at first, a bit scaly when old. The buds are ovoid with curved tips, dark purplish, often with grey hairs; the leaves are pinnate, up to 20cm (8in) long, with 9 to 17 toothed leaflets, dark green above, paler below with very variable autumn colours; they can be quite dull or lovely reds and gold. The white flowers are in dense corymbs, 8–15cm (3–6in) across, with woolly stems. There are several cul-

tivated varieties with different coloured berries and various leaf forms.

Kashmir rowan (*Sorbus cashmiriana*)
This lovely Indian species has pink flowers and white berries on pink stalks.

Hubei rowan (*Sorbus hupehensis*)
A Chinese tree with fairly pendulous grey-green leaves, glaucous beneath, white and pink berries, and more rounded flower corymbs than sargent's rowan (*Sorbus sargentiana*).

Swedish whitebeam
(Sorbus intermedia)
Native to Sweden, the Baltic States and Germany, this is very similar to the

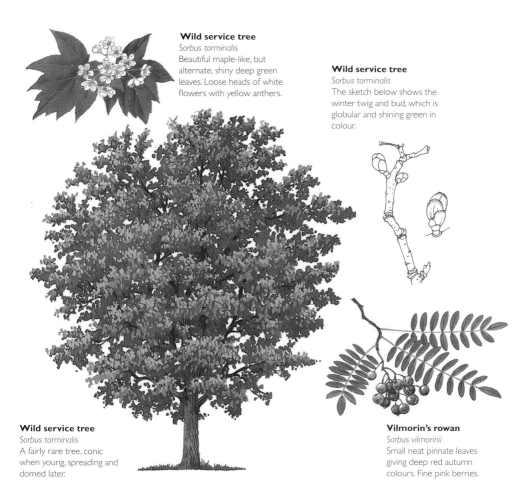

Wild service tree
Sorbus torminalis
Beautiful maple-like, but alternate, shiny deep green leaves. Loose heads of white flowers with yellow anthers.

Wild service tree
Sorbus torminalis
The sketch below shows the winter twig and bud, which is globular and shining green in colour.

Wild service tree
Sorbus torminalis
A fairly rare tree, conic when young, spreading and domed later.

Vilmorin's rowan
Sorbus vilmorinii
Small neat pinnate leaves giving deep red autumn colours. Fine pink berries.

whitebeam (*Sorbus aria*) but is smaller and narrower in form, has pinnately lobed leaves and larger berries.

Service tree of Fontainebleau (*Sorbus* x *latifolia*)

A hybrid between whitebeam (*Sorbus aria*) and wild service tree (*S. torminalis*), and intermediate between the two in appearance. Leaf shape and size, and berry shape and colour, are variable.

Sargent's rowan (*Sorbus sargentiana*)

A small, bushy Chinese tree with deep red buds, large pinnate leaves, up to 35cm (14in) long, tiny red berries and excellent gold and red autumn colours.

Wild service tree (*Sorbus torminalis*)

Native to Europe, this is a small dome-crowned tree with ovate alternate leaves, about 7 x 9cm (3 x 3½in), lobed like a maple leaf and doubly toothed, turning dark purple in autumn. White flowers, 1cm (½in) across, are grouped in rather loose corymbs, 6–9cm (2½–3½in) in diameter. The berries are reddish brown when ripe, obovoid, 1cm (½in) long, and quite sweet-tasting. The bark is fissured.

Vilmorin's rowan (*Sorbus vilmorinii*)

From China, this tree is distinguished by its smaller leaves, deep red autumn colours and beautiful pink berries.

Snowbell tree
Styrax japonica
Masses of slender-stalked white flowers hang from the twigs in late summer, just as the leaves emerge.

Snowbell tree
Styrax japonica
Mature leaf and long-stalked, small, round fruits held in a star-like calyx.

Snowbell tree
Styrax japonica
A dense, rounded broad crown with rather flat branches. Flowers in summer.

Snowbell Tree (*Styrax japonica*)

Snowbell trees, together with snow-drop trees (*Halesia monticola*), are among the few members of the storax family (Styracaceae) that grow to tree size. They provide the gardener with a range of fine trees that grow happily in a lime-free soil.

Snowbell tree (*Styrax japonica*)

A small, rounded, deciduous tree from China and Japan, the snowbell tree grows to a height of about 12m (40ft) and has a tendency to be broader than tall, with arching upper branches and almost level lower ones.

A special feature of the snowbell tree is the masses of bell-like white flowers on stalks, up to 4cm (1½in) long, hanging in small bunches along the branches in early summer, later developing into smooth, ovoid-globular fruits, about 1cm (½in) in diameter, silvery green and topped by a star-like green calyx, often with purple tops to its five rounded lobes. The leaves are alternate, shiny green, broadly elliptic and pointed, 4–8cm (1½–3in) long, and with a few remote teeth along their wavy margins. On mature trees, the bark is very attractive, with pinkish orange fissures between irregular grey ridges.

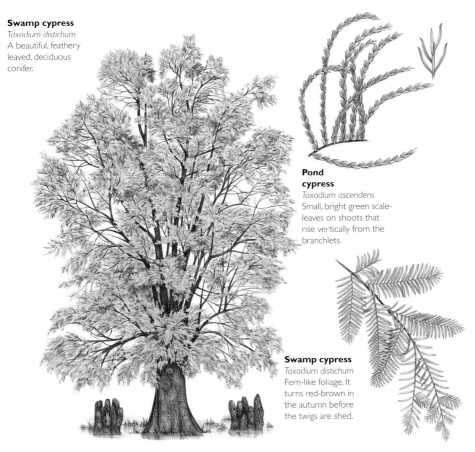

Swamp cypress
Taxodium distichum
A beautiful, feathery leaved, deciduous conifer.

Pond cypress
Taxodium ascendens
Small, bright green scale-leaves on shoots that rise vertically from the branchlets.

Swamp cypress
Taxodium distichum
Fern-like foliage. It turns red-brown in the autumn before the twigs are shed.

Deciduous Cypresses (*Taxodium*)

There are a few deciduous or semide-ciduous conifers from southern USA and Mexico which, instead of losing their leaves, shed lateral twigs in autumn.

Pond cypress (*Taxodium ascendens*)
This narrow tree, from Virginia to Alabama, has tufts and lines of neat little erect new shoots all along its twigs and branches. It is rather sparsely branched and open crowned, to 25m (80ft) tall, with a swollen trunk base. The leaves are scale-like, and only 4–8mm (⅙–⅜in) long.

Swamp or bald cypress
(*Taxodium distichum*)
Native to swamp areas in southern USA,

this grows to 45m (150ft) tall. The soft green foliage consists of fern-like sprays of slender linear leaves, about 12 x 2mm (½ x ¹⁄₁₆in), set alternately on twigs that are alternate on the branches. Male flowers are in the form of catkins, green at first, then turning purplish before shedding their pollen; the females are little green balls of bracts and scales. The cones are globular, 2–3cm (¾–1¼in) in diameter, with a few rather large scales with thickened edges, green ripening to purplish brown. The bark is reddish brown with many fissures, and the trunk often has large buttresses.

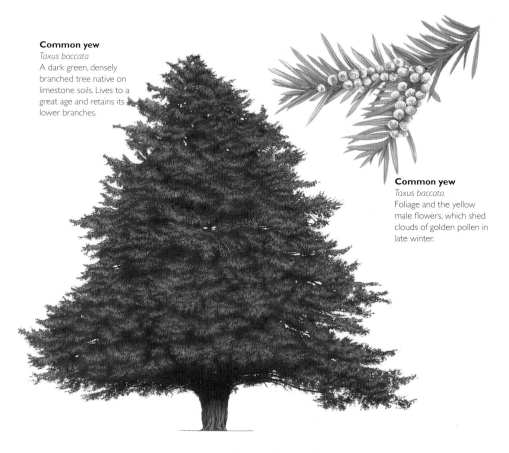

Common yew
Taxus baccata
A dark green, densely branched tree native on limestone soils. Lives to a great age and retains its lower branches.

Common yew
Taxus baccata
Foliage and the yellow male flowers, which shed clouds of golden pollen in late winter.

Yew *(Taxus)*

The yews *(Taxus)* comprise about half a dozen species, with many variations within each one, very widely distributed across the northern hemisphere and distinguished from true conifers by their single seeds being enclosed in a fleshy cup or 'aril'.

Common yew *(Taxus baccata)*
This tree is one of the most common and best-known hardy evergreens. It is native to Europe, Algeria, Asia Minor, Iran and the Himalayas, preferring limestone soils.

It is the species most widely planted in churchyards, hence it has acquired an unfair dismal image; to appreciate its real charm, one should see it in its native chalk downland.

Yews live longer than any other tree in Europe, and it is likely that a few may have reached almost 1,500 years and quite a number over 1,000 years, although local figures are often exaggerated, and should be treated with caution.

The trunks reach quite large dimensions, many are between 2 and 4m (6 and 12ft) in diameter, but great heights are not reached. Almost all of the large yews are hollow. The trunks are usually deeply fluted, often sprouting several side shoots, and the reddish brown bark

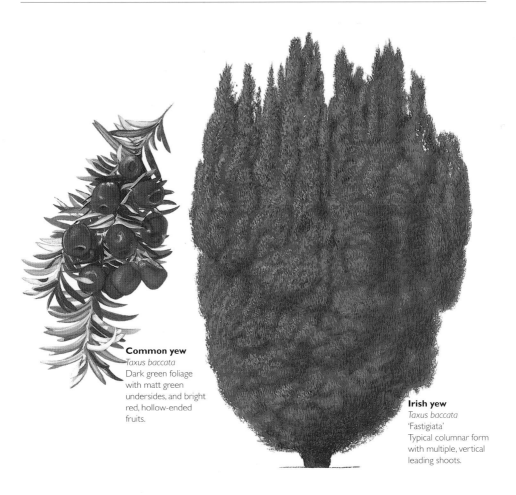

Common yew
Taxus baccata
Dark green foliage
with matt green
undersides, and bright
red, hollow-ended
fruits.

Irish yew
Taxus baccata
'Fastigiata'
Typical columnar form
with multiple, vertical
leading shoots.

scales away, leaving irregular patches of
dark red and fawn. Normal leaves are
2–4cm (¾–1½in) long x 2–3mm (¹⁄₁₆–⅛in)
wide, linear, abruptly narrowing to a
point, very dark green above, matt dull
green below, set spirally on erect shoots
but in two flat ranks on the side shoots.
The masses of male flowers look like
little beads; the females are usually on
separate trees, small, green and pear
shaped. The beautiful berries or 'arils',
enclosing the dark poisonous seed, are
bright red when ripe.

There are many cultivars of yew,
examples being golden yew, silver yew,
weeping yew and dwarf yew, but perhaps
the best-known one is Irish Yew, 'Fastigiata', a compact columnar tree with all
branches almost erect, and very dark
green leaves set all round the shoots.
This cultivar is always female and is very
widely planted, especially in churchyards
and gardens. 'Aurea' is a golden type.

Japanese yew *(Taxus cuspidata)*
A broad, bushy tree from Japan with
hard spine-tipped leaves, 2–4cm
(¾–1½in) long, turned sharply upwards,
dark green above, brownish yellow
below. The berries are paler than those
of common yew *(Taxus baccata)*.

Western red cedar
Thuja plicata
A splendid tree of narrow
conic form with dense
shiny green foliage and
reddish brown bark.

Western red cedar
Thuja plicata
Foliage deep green above,
paler beneath with white
streaks.

Thujas (*Thuja*)

Thujas are often referred as cedars, but are more accurately known by their botanical name, thujas (the name cedar should really only be used for *Cedrus* species).

White cedar (*Thuja occidentalis*)
This close relation to western red cedar (*Thuja plicata*) occurs in eastern Canada and northeastern USA. It is much smaller, growing only to about 20m (70ft). The scale-like leaves are smaller, less shiny, more flattened, paler green and without the white marks on the lower surface of *T. plicata*; the cones have only four large scales instead of six.

Western red cedar (*Thuja plicata*)
This is a splendid tree from the West coast and northern Rocky Mountains of North America, to 60m (200ft) tall. The overlapping scale-like leaves are aromatic when bruised, shiny dark green above, whitish streaked below. Both male and female flowers are small and yellowish. The cones have six large scales with tips spreading as small spines. The bark is reddish brown, soft and lifts off in strips. On old, open-grown trees, the lower branches sometimes layer and form rings of vertical boles all around the mother trunk.

170

American basswood
Tilia americana
The largest-leafed lime.
Leaves are yellow-green.

Limes (*Tilia*)

There are about 30 species of *Tilia* in the northern temperate zone; several of them are native in eastern USA, but none in western North America.

The particular characteristics of limes are their tough, fibrous inner bark, heart-shaped leaves, which are oblique at the base, flowers in cymes, from a stalk midway along a large membraneous bract, and buds with only two visible scales, one much larger than the other. Lime tree flowers are strongly scented and a great attraction for bees; lime honey is well known.

Interbreeding has given rise to much confusion over the naming of varieties, but the following notes cover a few of the better-known trees.

American basswood
(*Tilia americana* syn. *T. glabra*)
Up to 40m (130ft), this fine tree, native to Canada and the USA, has very large leaves, sometimes as much as 30 x 20cm (12 x 8in). The fruiting stem bracts are large, up to 12 x 3cm (5 x 1¼in); the fruits are thick-shelled and without any marked ribs.

Small-leafed lime
(*Tilia cordata* syn. *T. parvifolia*)
Native to Europe, this slightly smaller

171

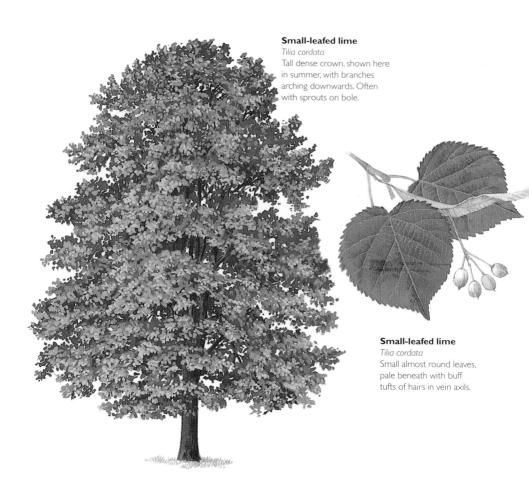

Small-leafed lime
Tilia cordata
Tall dense crown, shown here
in summer, with branches
arching downwards. Often
with sprouts on bole.

Small-leafed lime
Tilia cordata
Small almost round leaves,
pale beneath with buff
tufts of hairs in vein axils.

tree is good where space is restricted. It is comparatively slow growing and reaches a maximum height of 32m (105ft), with a tall, dense, irregular crown. It flowers late in the season; the fruits are thin-shelled and smooth. Its leaves are slightly smaller than those of the common lime, rounded, more glaucous, and with orange or buff tufts in the vein axils on the undersurface.

Common lime

(Tilia × europaea syn. *T. vulgaris)*
A natural hybrid between *Tilia platyphyllos* and *T. cordata*, this is the commonest lime in Britain and is also widespread in the rest of Europe. A fine tree, the tallest broadleaved species in Britain, reaching 45m (150ft), and living to a great age, anything from 500 to around 1,000 years. It is a graceful tree with a tall billowing crown formed of branches that first ascend and then arch over. It has long been a great favourite for garden training and many very old avenues can be found.

The ovoid red-brown buds open to unfurl heart-shaped leaves, 6–10cm (2½–4in) long, broad but with short-pointed tips, sharply serrate and smooth except for small whitish tufts in the main

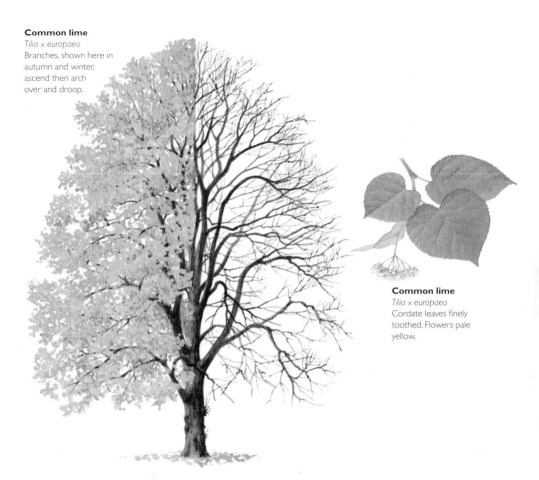

Common lime
Tilia × europaea
Branches, shown here in autumn and winter, ascend then arch over and droop.

Common lime
Tilia × europaea
Cordate leaves finely toothed. Flowers pale yellow.

axils on the lower surface. The pendent, yellowish white flowers, four to ten together, are very fragrant and ripen into hard, broadly ovoid fruits, 6–8mm (¼–⅜in) in diameter, which are faintly ribbed and pubescent.

The bark on old trees is fissured into a network of shallow ridges, and the lower bole is commonly covered in burrs and dense thickets of small shoots.

Oliver's lime *(Tilia oliveri)*

Closely related to *Tilia tomentosa*, this fine Chinese tree is one of the best limes and deserves wider use. It grows to 25m (80ft) tall, with fairly straight ascending branches and a high-domed crown. The large leaves, up to 14 x 12cm (5½ x 5in), are pointed at the tip, evenly cordate at the base, with small, whitish, pointed teeth and bright silvery undersides. Branch scars are dark curved folds.

Pendent silver lime *(Tilia petiolaris)*

Of doubtful origin, but probably from eastern Europe, *Tilia petiolaris* is a beautiful tree with rather sinuous ascending branches and graceful pendent branchlets. It is usually grafted and forms a narrow-domed crown, reaching up to about 32m (105ft).

The leaves are deeply cordate on slen-

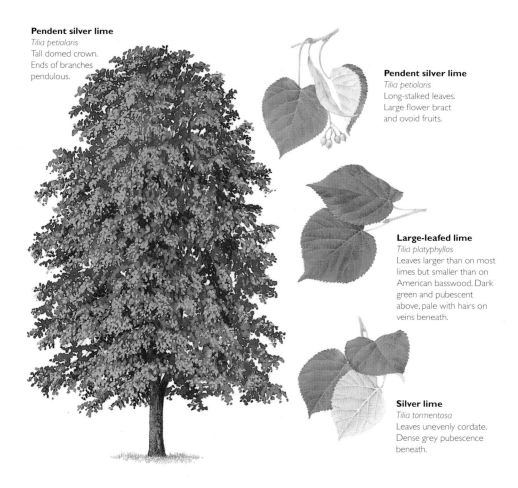

Pendent silver lime
Tilia petiolaris
Tall domed crown.
Ends of branches
pendulous.

Pendent silver lime
Tilia petiolaris
Long-stalked leaves.
Large flower bract
and ovoid fruits.

Large-leafed lime
Tilia platyphyllos
Leaves larger than on most
limes but smaller than on
American basswood. Dark
green and pubescent
above, pale with hairs on
veins beneath.

Silver lime
Tilia tormentosa
Leaves unevenly cordate.
Dense grey pubescence
beneath.

der, white pubescent stalks, and have white undersides.

Large-leafed lime *(Tilia platyphyllos)*
Native to Europe and Asia Minor, growing to 40m (130ft) tall, with a narrow-domed crown and branches more ascending than in common lime, this is usually a clean and shapely tree; its straight clean trunk seldom has sprouts at the base.

The leaves are variable, from 8–16cm (3–6in) across, deeply cordate, crenate and serrate, dark green, sometimes but not always pubescent on upper surfaces, pale green and densely pubescent on the veins beneath. The flowers grow in bunches of three to five, and the flowering stalk bracts are large and whitish green; the fruits are 8–10mm (⅜–½in) in diameter, prominently five-ribbed and densely pubescent.

There is a cut-leaved cultivar known as 'Laciniata' or 'Aspleniifolia'.

Silver or white lime *(Tilia tomentosa)*
A fine broad-domed tree, up to 30m (100ft) tall, with steeply ascending branches, native to southeast Europe and southwest Asia. Its special features are the white woolly young shoots and the dense, silvery grey pubescence on the back of the almost round leaves.

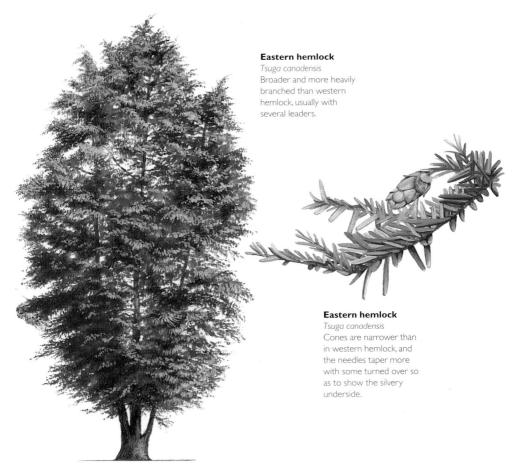

Eastern hemlock
Tsuga canadensis
Broader and more heavily
branched than western
hemlock, usually with
several leaders.

Eastern hemlock
Tsuga canadensis
Cones are narrower than
in western hemlock, and
the needles taper more
with some turned over so
as to show the silvery
underside.

Hemlocks (*Tsuga*)

Originating from North America, east Asia and the Himalayas, there are nine species in this small coniferous genus, closely related to the spruces (*Picea*). The group includes one important timber tree (*Tsuga heterophylla*), and several good ornamentals.

The common name 'hemlock' is unfortunate because their only likeness to the poisonous umbelliferous herb is that the crushed foliage of some of them has a similar scent (trees in the genus *Tsuga* are not at all poisonous).

Eastern hemlock *(Tsuga canadensis)*
This is a smaller and more bushy species than western hemlock (*Tsuga heterophylla*), and originates from Canada and eastern USA. Its needles taper more than those of western hemlock and some of those on the top side of the shoots often twist so that the silver bands are uppermost. The cones are similar but rather smaller than those of western hemlock.

Carolina hemlock *(Tsuga caroliniana)*
Another American species, from the Allegheny mountains, this has a broad pyramidal form and dense branches with upswept tips. The glossy green needles are slender, 1–2cm (½–¾in) long, and set at irregular angles to the stems.

Chinese hemlock
Tsuga chinensis
Has sparser leaves than western hemlock, with greenish bands on the lower side rather than white. The small shoots are more nodding.

Western hemlock
Tsuga heterophylla
A most graceful tree, with beautiful foliage and delicate pendulous small shoots. Branches are relatively thin and the lower, older ones tend to droop.

Northern Japanese hemlock
Tsuga diversifolia
Has shorter, stouter leaves than the others, with very bright silver lines beneath.

Chinese hemlock *(Tsuga chinensis)*
Originating from central and west China, where it grows up to 30m (100ft) tall, this is rather similar to the western hemlock *(Tsuga heterophylla)* in form and foliage, but with rather larger and rounder cones.

Northern Japanese hemlock
(Tsuga diversifolia)
From Northern Japan, this has shorter, shinier leaves than the other hemlocks, with silver bands on the undersides.

Himalayan hemlock
(Tsuga dumosa syn. *T. brunoniana)*
Tsuga dumosa is a tall, graceful, pendulous-branched tree from the eastern Himalayas, which grows up to 35m (120ft) tall. It has slender needles, up to 3cm (1¼in) long, with broad silver bands on the underside. It is a tender species, only succeeding in mild areas.

Western hemlock *(Tsuga heterophylla)*
The largest, best-known and most valuable timber species, this is a giant North American tree, often over 60m (200ft) tall. It is one of the most beautiful of all the conifers, of narrowly conical form, with slender, rather pendulous shoots and flat needles, parted on each side of the shoot, green above but with two bright silver bands beneath, and of vari-

Mountain hemlock
Tsuga mertensiana
A beautiful narrow-form
tree with spire-like top and
grey-green foliage.

Mountain hemlock
Tsuga mertensiana
Needles point forwards
and are set radially round
the shoots, grey or silvery
green on both surfaces.

Western hemlock
Tsuga heterophylla
Leaves are short, dark
green on top, with two
silver bands beneath.
Cones are small and
pendulous on the ends of
the shoots, with only a few
leathery scales.

able length. It makes an excellent hedge.

The small, globular male flowers are red at first but yellow when the pollen is shed, and the females are purple ovoids, about 6mm (¼in) long. Cones, often very numerous, are pendulous on the ends of small shoots, bluntly ovoid, 2–3cm (¾–1¼in) long with a few leathery scales, green at first but pale brown when ripe. The seeds are extremely small.

Western hemlock bark is very rich in tannin and has been extensively used in the leather industry; it is smooth at first but on older trees becomes shallowly fissured into irregular small plates.

Mountain hemlock

(Tsuga mertensiana syn. *T. hookeriana, T. pattoniana)*

A beautiful high-elevation tree from western North America, this grows up to 45m (150ft) tall, of narrow form with a spire-like top and dense uneven-length branches with drooping small twigs.

The needles, 1.5–2.5cm (½–1in) long, set radially on the shoots, are usually grey-green all over, but on some trees, such as 'Glauca', they are of a beautiful blue-grey hue. The cones are spruce-like and much larger than those of any other hemlock, often up to 7cm (3in) long.

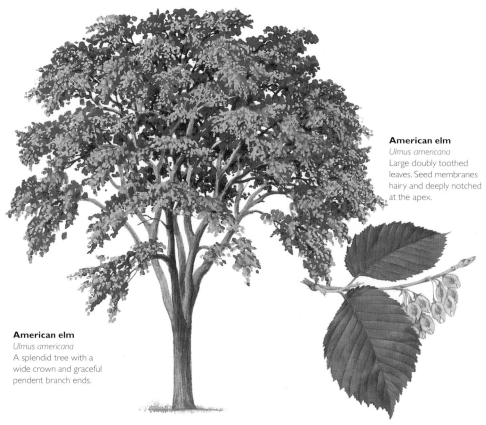

American elm
Ulmus americana
Large doubly toothed
leaves. Seed membranes
hairy and deeply notched
at the apex.

American elm
Ulmus americana
A splendid tree with a
wide crown and graceful
pendent branch ends.

Elms (*Ulmus*)

There are about 20 species of this genus in the northern temperate regions but as there are many hybrids and special clones, exact identification is difficult. Only a few of the best-known examples can be dealt with here.

All elms have alternate leaves, usually rough to the touch, lop-sided at the base, and almost all are deciduous. In some species the twigs tend to develop corky winged ridges.

A point of special interest is that several species only rarely produce fertile seeds and are propagated instead by sucker growth, so their characteristics do not vary by cross-fertilization and their offspring are remarkably uniform. The development of prolific suckers from the roots makes elms particularly suitable for hedgerows, because they can be constantly increased without replanting. With their large crowns they are also good shade trees, and nearly all elms yield valuable timber.

Tragically the so-called Dutch elm disease has devastated the elms in a number of countries.

American white elm (*Ulmus americana*)
A splendid tree widely used in America, this is equal in size to wych elm (*Ulmus*

Wheatley elm
Ulmus carpinifolia var. *sarniensis*
A fine, narrow-form tree, very suitable for street and town planting.

glabra) but the branches are gracefully pendulous, and the leaves are longer and more pointed, with long stalks.

Cornish elm
(Ulmus carpinifolia var. cornubiensis syn. U. stricta)

When young, this variety is very like Wheatley elm (*Ulmus carpinifolia* var. *sarniensis*) though not so dense; in later life its rather sparse ascending branches become rounded at the top, giving the tree a narrow fan-like form with little foliage except near the branch ends.

'Wredei' is a golden-leaved cultivar with small shiny leaves.

Wheatley or Jersey elm
(Ulmus carpinifolia var. sarniensis syn. Ulmus wheatleyi)

This tree has a narrow-pointed pyramidal form, with numerous steeply ascending branches.

There is a golden-leaved cultivar, 'Aurea', sometimes called 'Dicksonii'.

Wych elm *(Ulmus glabra)*

This native of Britain and western Asia has a wider, more-rounded outline than English elm (*Ulmus procera*), with a less definite main stem and more arching branches; the bark is smoother, with longer, shallower fissures. The buds are

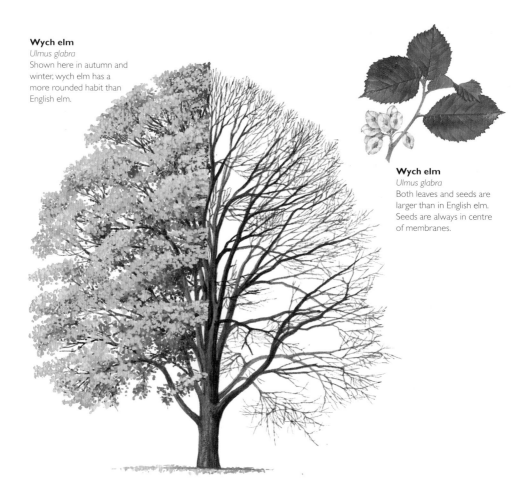

Wych elm
Ulmus glabra
Shown here in autumn and winter, wych elm has a more rounded habit than English elm.

Wych elm
Ulmus glabra
Both leaves and seeds are larger than in English elm. Seeds are always in centre of membranes.

darker and a little larger (up to 15cm/ 6in). Wych elm seldom produces sucker growth but its comparatively larger seeds are very fertile.

'Camperdownii' (camperdown elm) is a common, grafted, weeping cultivar with large leaves, as much as 20 x 12cm (8 x 5in), and a broad head of spreading tortuous branches.

Dutch elm hybrids *(Ulmus × hollandica)*
This large group of hybrids between *Ulmus glabra* and *U. carpinifolia* is widely used in Europe. Two of the best known are described below.

'Vegeta' (Huntingdon elm) is similar to Dutch elm in size. It has straighter and more steeply ascending branches and leaves with long stalks. The flowers are larger and later than those of most elms.

'Hollandica' syn. *Ulmus major* (Dutch elm) is a large tree, up to 40m (130ft) high, with a wide open crown and somewhat pendulous branch ends. It shoots suckers both from roots and the upper surface of old branches. The leaves are large, up to 15 x 8cm (6 x 3in), and have a rough texture.

Chinese elm *(Ulmus parvifolia)*
A native of China, Japan and Korea, this evergreen or semi-evergreen tree, which

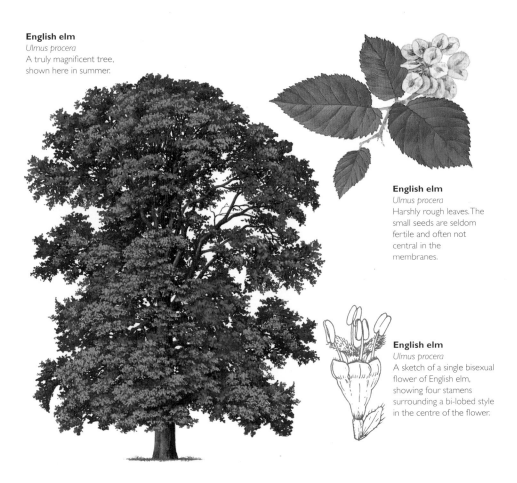

English elm
Ulmus procera
A truly magnificent tree,
shown here in summer.

English elm
Ulmus procera
Harshly rough leaves. The
small seeds are seldom
fertile and often not
central in the
membranes.

English elm
Ulmus procera
A sketch of a single bisexual
flower of English elm,
showing four stamens
surrounding a bi-lobed style
in the centre of the flower.

flowers in autumn, has very small, fairly narrow leaves, 3–4cm (1¼–1⅓in) long.

English elm

(Ulmus procera syn. *Ulmus campestris)*
A magnificent, tall, stately tree, up to 40m (130ft) high, with girths to 7m (22ft) or more; it develops a large-domed crown with lesser domes on the ends of large ascending branches. Unfortunately it is not very deep-rooted and is therefore liable to be thrown by gales, especially on wet sites. The English elm, once very popular, has been widely planted throughout Europe and America.

The small, ovoid, dark brown winter buds are only 2–3mm (up to ⅛in) long. The darkish green leaves are doubly toothed, with a very rough upper surface, and strongly marked parallel veins; they are lopsided at the base, variable in shape and size, 4–8cm (1½–3in) long, and usually fairly orbicular but shortly pointed. The red stamens of the small flowers massed on the bare twigs give a crimson haze against the sky in late winter/early spring, developing later into bunches of small infertile seeds, each near the tip of a round green membrane.

The dark, grey-brown bark is deeply fissured into short irregular plates.

Caucasian zelkova
Zelkova carpinifolia
Unique, huge ovoid crown, shown here
in summer and winter, formed of
steeply ascending branches springing
from a very short bole.

Caucasian zelkova
Zelkova carpinifolia
Elliptic, crenate, sub-sessile
leaves and tiny, round,
green female flowers.

Zelkovas *(Zelkova)*

A small group of broadleaved deciduous trees from East Asia, Crete and
the Caucasus, the zelkovas are closely
related to the elms (*Ulmus*) but fortunately less liable to Dutch elm disease —
though not completely immune.

Caucasian zelkova

(Zelkova carpinifolia syn. *Z. crenata)*
This tree from the Caucasus mountains
is perhaps the best known, growing up to
35m (120ft), with a short beech-like
trunk that usually divides into a mass of
long, steeply ascending branches, creat-
ing a high oblong-oval bush shape. The
bark is rather like beech (*Fagus*) but
peels off in flakes revealing small orange-
pink patches. The timber is tough,
durable and of good quality but is rarely
exported; the form of the tree prevents
any long large balks. The alternate, acute
elliptical leaves, up to 12 x 6cm (5 x
2½in), are crenate and toothed, almost
sessile, dark green above with scattered
hairs, pale green beneath, and downy,
especially near the veins, turning to
orange-brown in the autumn. The flow-

Cut-leafed zelkova
Zelkova verschaffeltii
Remarkable long, coarse, pointed teeth on leaves that are rough above, pubescent beneath.

Keaki
Zelkova serrata
Larger leaves with mucronate teeth. Good yellow, orange and pink autumn colours.

ers are small, greenish and inconspicuous, the fruit the size of a small pea with narrow ribs.

Keaki or Japanese zelkova
(*Zelkova serrata* syn. *Z. acuminata*)

A much valued timber tree in Japan and Korea, growing to 35m (120ft), this has low, arching branches forming a broad, round-topped crown. The wood is often beautifully grained and used for quality furniture and cabinet work.

The leaves are sharply toothed, instead of crenate, more acutely pointed, and tend to be pendulous. Autumn shades are very fine — mixed yellows, pinks and oranges.

Chinese zelkova
(*Zelkova sinica*)

This species is remarkable for its orange-pink bark, zigzag twigs and uncut leaves.

Cut-leafed zelkova
(*Zelkova verschaffeltii*)

Probably of Caucasian origin, the special feature of this species is its sharply acute toothed edges of the leaves, cut much more deeply than in other zelkovas.

Leaf Types

LEAF SHAPES

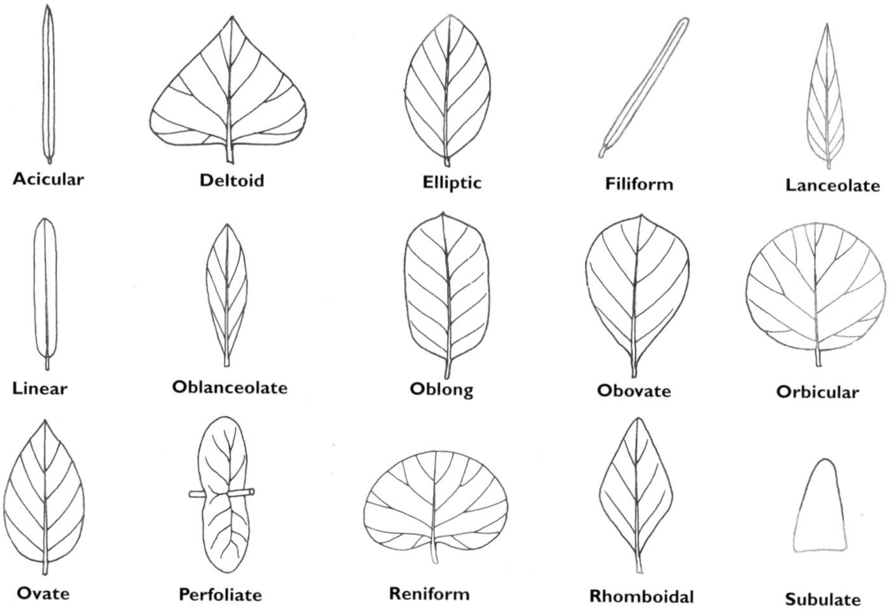

Acicular

Deltoid

Elliptic

Filiform

Lanceolate

Linear

Oblanceolate

Oblong

Obovate

Orbicular

Ovate

Perfoliate

Reniform

Rhomboidal

Subulate

LEAF MARGINS

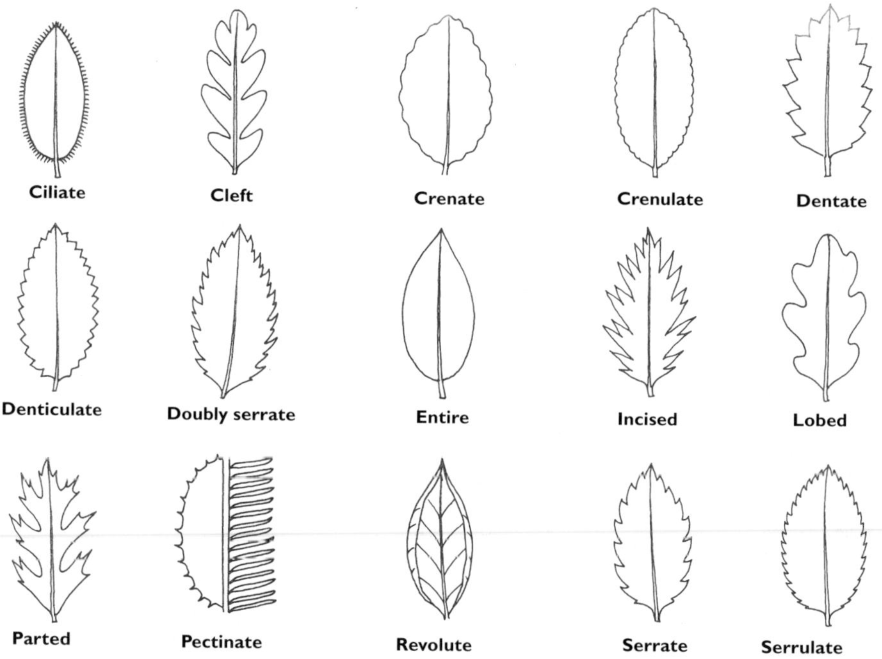

Ciliate

Cleft

Crenate

Crenulate

Dentate

Denticulate

Doubly serrate

Entire

Incised

Lobed

Parted

Pectinate

Revolute

Serrate

Serrulate

LEAF TIPS

Acute **Acuminate** **Aristate** **Cuspidate** **Emarginate** **Mucronate** **Obtuse** **Retuse**

LEAF BASES

Attenuate **Auriculate** **Cordate** **Cuneate** **Hastate** **Oblique** **Obtuse** **Sagittate** **Truncate**

INFLORESCENCES

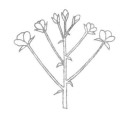  

Corymb
Dome-shaped or flat flower head in which the outer flowers open first.

Cyme
Convex inflorescence with inner flowers opening first.

Raceme
Narrow flower head with lowest buds opening first.

Spike
Similar to a raceme but the flowers are without stalks.

Umbel
Flattish flower head with stalks from the same point.

Panicle
Raceme which is made up of a number of smaller racemes.

PRUNING EFFECTS

Coppiced
At intervals the tree is cropped to ground level to make it yield small branches.

Pollarded
At regular intervals the tree is cut back to make it yield a number of small branches.

LEAF TYPES

Bipinnate **Pinnate** **Palmate** **Compound palmate (digitate)** **Trifoliolate**

Glossary

Afforestation To cover land with trees, usually to yield timber but sometimes to give shelter, conserve moisture or stop erosion.

Angiosperm A class of plants whose seeds are borne within the walls of an ovary.

Adpressed/Appressed Closely pressed to an adjoining member, such as bud to a twig.

Axil The upper angle between a leaf stalk and a twig, a twig and a branch or a leaf vein and the midrib.

Axillary Within that angle.

Bark The outer layer of a tree that protects the inner tissues from damage and disease.

Bast The soft, often fibrous, layer of phloem tissue between the bark and the inner cells.

Bole The trunk of a tree, usually the lower section.

Bract A leaf-like structure beneath a flower or at the base of a stalk. Often seen on conifer cones.

Broadleaved tree Often called hardwoods and usually with broader leaves than conifers, this large group, mostly dicotyledons, all belong to the group of plants called Angiosperms.

Cambium A layer of active cell division that produces new tissues, such as the vascular cambium that gives rise to new xylem and phloem tissue.

Catkin A dense spike of scaly-bracted, stalkless flowers. Usually drooping.

Coniferous tree Often called softwoods and usually with needle-like leaves, these trees belong to the primitive group of plants called Gymnosperms ('naked seeded'). They have woody fruit bodies called cones.

Copse A small wood.

Cork A layer of dead cells on the outside of a stem or root that guards the inner tissues against damage and desiccation. Well developed in the cork oak.

Cotyledon The first leaves that emerge from the seed.

Cultivar Cultivated varieties that are propagated, not by seeds, but by cuttings or grafting.

Cuticle The varnish-like impervious coating of an epidermis that prevents damage and water loss.

Dicotyledon A plant having two cotyledons. One of two major subdivisions of flowering plants.

Dioecious Having male and female flowers on separate plants.

Epidermis The surface layer of cells just below the cuticle.

Epiphyte A plant growing upon another for support only.

Exserted Projecting visibly from between other parts.

Glabrous Without hairs.

Glaucous Silvery or bluish-grey. Also, with a waxy bloom.

Growth ring The annual ring of growth by which a tree increases its diameter.

Gymnosperm A class of primitive plants that are 'naked seeding', their seeds being exposed on a scale and not concealed in an ovary.

Heartwood The darker, drier central core of wood in a tree. It contains no living cells and is more durable than the outer sapwood.

Hybrid A cross between two different species.

Lamina The blade of a leaf.

Layering The establishment of a new plant when a branch makes contact with the ground and sends roots into the soil.

Leaflet A single member of a compound or pinnate leaf.

Lenticel A breathing pore that shows as a corky or white mark on trunks and branches.

Liana A woody climbing plant with long, rope-like stems.

Lignin The chemical substance impregnated in the cell walls of xylem tissue and giving wood its basic characteristics.

Medullary ray A sheet of tissue running radially through a stem or root and responsible for transport of materials across the stem. Seen as silvery lines in some timbers. Very clear in oak timber.

Mesophyll The inner tissue of a leaf.

Monocotyledon A plant having one cotyledon. One of two major subdivisions of flowering plants.

Monoecious Having separate male and female flowers on the same plant.

Parasite A plant living at the expense of another organism.

Petiole A leaf stalk.

Phloem Vascular tissue that transports food materials made by the plant. Often called bast.

Photosynthesis The process by which carbohydrates are synthesized from carbon dioxide and water in the presence of sunlight and chlorophyll.

Phyllode A flattened stem that looks and functions like a leaf.

Pneumatophore An aerial root that grows vertically upwards to provide roots submerged in water or mud with essential air.

Podocarps A family of evergreen conifers occurring mainly in the southern hemisphere. They have male and female flowers usually on separate trees and characteristic stalked fruits.

Pollination The transfer of pollen from the male parts of a flower (anther) to the female part (stigma).

Pubescent Hairy.

Radicle The first root developing from a seed.

Reflexed Turned back sharply.

Relict A primitive survivor from earlier times; a 'living fossil'.

Resin The sticky 'sap' exuded by many conifers.

Respiration The reverse of photosynthesis, whereby some organic matter is broken down to carbon dioxide and water, with the release of energy.

Roundwood Timber in the form of logs before being sawn into boards.

Rubber The elastic substance made from the sap or 'latex' of rubber trees.

Sapling A young tree.

Sapwood The newly formed, light-coloured wood that forms the outer region of a tree trunk. It is composed of living xylem cells that transport water throughout the tree.

Scale A small leaf or bract. The term is loosely applied to many structures, such as bud scale, cone scale, and so on.

Sessile Without a stalk.

Silviculture The care of woods, usually for the production of timber. Arboriculture is the care of individual trees.

Springwood The paler and less dense wood formed in spring and early summer. Also called earlywood.

Stand A continuous growth or plantation of trees. Usually applied to one species.

Stave One of a number of curved strips of wood that make up a barrel.

Stomata Breathing pores, found mainly on the under-surface of leaves.

Stratification The grouping of vegetation into well defined layers, such as trees, shrubs and ground vegetation.

Sucker A shoot arising from below soil level close to the parent plant.

Summerwood Wood formed during the summer, usually recognizable as the darker and denser portion of the annual growth ring. Also called latewood.

Sustained yield A term used in forestry for the ideal situation in which timber can be produced in commercially useful quantities year after year.

Taiga Primeval Siberian forest. The term is also used in a general sense for the coniferous forest that stretches across the northern hemisphere.

Tannin An acidic substance distilled from the bark of oak and some other trees and used for converting hide into leather.

Taproot A stout, vertical, anchoring root developed from the radicle.

Transpiration The loss of water from a plant by evaporation, especially through the stomata.

Tree line The elevation at which tree growth ceases. Most clearly seen where coniferous forest clothes mountainsides.

Uniform stand A plantation of trees of similar size and age.

Unisexual Of one sex only.

Variety A subdivision of a species. The term is used mainly for natural variation within a species rather than for new plants produced by cultivation, for which cultivar is more appropriate.

Vascular tissue The tissue system in plants that conducts water and food substances and gives mechanical support. It is composed mainly of xylem (wood) and phloem (bast).

Veneer A very thin sheet of wood cut from a rotating log. Veneers are used as surface decoration on a wide variety of board products.

Vivipary The production of seeds that germinate while still on the parent plant.

Wane The rough edge of a timber board remaining after a log has been cut but before it is trimmed. Fences made of such untrimmed boards are often called wany lap.

Whorl A ring of structures, such as leaves or flowers, arising from the same level.

Xerophyte A plant adapted to living in very dry conditions.

Xylem The basic tissue of wood, consisting of long cells with thickened walls and responsible for transporting water and mineral salts throughout the tree.

INDEX